# FIVE-YEAR MILLIONAIRE

*A Roadmap for Investing in the Stock Market, Wealth Accumulation, and Financial Independence*

## JASON BROWN

Stock Market Coach and Options Trader

To my mother, Zolda Brown. You always preached the importance of education. You instilled in my brother and me that education is the key to leveling up in this life and that earning a degree was something that no one could ever take away from us. You made sure my brother and I had a roof over our heads and food in our bellies. You took us to church and made sure we got to school by any means and that our homework was always done. You were one of the hardest working, most selfless examples of a true Christian woman that I have ever seen. Because of who you are at your core, your love, your giving spirit, I am who I am today. Thank you for the sacrificial life you lived and the unconditional love you gave.

To my aunt Lois A. Flagg, who was an educator in Mississippi. You instilled the importance of education into my mother. You didn't value money, clothes, cars, homes, or jewelry; you valued education. You poured your heart, soul, and knowledge into the community and educated generations of children and families. For that, a library was named after you, the Lois A. Flagg Library. Now, because of what you instilled in my mother, which was passed down to me, perhaps one day my book can sit on shelves of libraries across the world.

# Table of Contents

Dear Reader — 1

**CHAPTER 1** "What Do They Do?" Houses — 3

**CHAPTER 2** Down But Not Out — 21

**CHAPTER 3** Power Charts, Power Trades, Power Profits — 39

**CHAPTER 4** You Never Go Broke Taking a Profit — 59

**CHAPTER 5** Is the Stock Market a Scam? — 81

**CHAPTER 6** The Stock Market Doesn't Care That Rent Is Due Next Week — 97

**CHAPTER 7** The Five-Year Millionaire Plan — 111

**CHAPTER 8** Protecting Your "Ass"ets — 131

**CHAPTER 9** The Path and Tools to Success — 147

Conclusion — 163

Acknowledgments — 167

# Dear Reader,

This is the book I wish I'd had when I first became curious about the stock market as a teenager and had no one to coach me. It's the book I wish I'd had while I taught myself how to invest and learned from the school of hard knocks—and I mean hard. Early on, I made some bad beginner mistakes and lost everything. I learned from those mistakes. I started again, slowly and carefully this time, understanding what I had done wrong and unlocking the matrix of how to do it right.

Today I am a millionaire living in my lakefront dream home, and I am the founder of The Brown Report and Power Trades University where I help new investors and traders learn to do things right. Through my online platform, I offer courses, coaching, and a community for those who are or want to become responsible and knowledgeable investors and traders, and I provide a roadmap to becoming a millionaire in five years from the stock market.

The same sound investment principles that I teach in my programs will unlock the matrix for you too, whether you're feeling stuck in your investing journey, getting frustrated with the stock market, or wondering how you'll ever get ahead with investing.

- The secret to understanding the best times to buy and sell stocks.
- How to put the odds in your favor regardless of which direction stocks are going.
- How to protect your account and make a profit in the short and medium terms.

You'll not only discover how it's possible to become a millionaire in about the time it takes to get a college degree, but you'll learn how to protect your account from major losses along the way. Regardless of your current career, financial situation, available free time, or knowledge of investing, the strategies I will share with you can literally change your life.

Take it from someone who started with nothing, lost everything, and came out on top. I've done the hard work for you and now it's your turn to benefit.

Cheers! You're a few chapters away from starting your journey toward becoming a millionaire.

*Jason Brown*

**CHAPTER 1**

# "What Do They Do?" Houses

When I first made **$113K** in the stock market in a single year, I decided it was time to buy something I'd always wanted—a really nice car. My cousin, who was a trader and had made over six figures in the stock market, had bought himself a brand-new Cadillac Escalade. He thought it was time I leveled up my car game.

"We're traders now, we need to look the part," my cousin said.

I wasn't sure about buying a car, let alone a high-end luxury car. I'd never had that kind of money. I was happy with my upgraded living situation—a nice condo apartment without bars on the windows in the suburbs. But eventually, my cousin convinced me to go to a Lexus dealership for a test drive. "Let's go and take a look."

When we got there, I was still hesitant. They ran my credit, which

I knew was good. I had the money in the bank but even after getting approved, I wasn't sure I wanted to commit to buying a car. We'd had a couple of good years trading but there was a voice in my head asking if we could maintain it, wondering if we'd simply been lucky and whether I could handle a long-term financial commitment.

"I'm leaving," my cousin told me. "I'm not coming back to pick you up because you're driving home in your new Lexus. You only live once," he repeated for the thousandth time.

So, I told the sales rep, "All right, ring it up. I'm taking the Lexus home."

This is how little I knew about buying a new car—the one I test drove was the one they washed, gassed up, and prepared for me to drive home.

"Oh, I thought you were going to bring a new one around with zero miles," I said.

The sales rep looked at me strangely. "This is a brand-new car."

It only had about 100 miles on it. The rep explained that those miles came from moving the car onto and off the trailer, driving it to park it and a few short test drives. I can only imagine what was going through his head. He shared with me that he and his co-workers couldn't afford to drive one of those cars, yet here he was selling one to someone who didn't even understand the process of buying a new car.

I bought the Lexus and drove it home feeling like a champion. It didn't stop there. Later in the week I spent another $2,500 on 20-inch rims. I couldn't believe I was finally able to afford the car of my dreams and accessorize it the way I wanted to. I was living and riding high on life and high off the stock market.

Life wasn't so bad, after all, for a kid who grew up poor and ran with gangs with a Detroit public school education.

## I DIDN'T KNOW WE WERE POOR

Growing up, my brother and I slept in California Raisin sleeping bags, inspired by a fictional, animated music group from the 80s. In my childhood home, only the adults had beds, but I didn't know I was poor because we lived in a neighborhood where all the houses had bars on the windows and that seemed normal. Why we and everybody around us lived in houses like that wasn't something I thought about.

It wasn't until I visited one of my friends for a sleepover and saw his bed that I began to grasp my family's financial status. "Whoa, you have a bed!" I said. "Yeah, of course I have a bed," my friend said. I thought a) he's an only child, and b) he comes from a two-parent, two-income household. Maybe that's why they were able to get him a bed. For the first time in my life I realized, "Okay, we're poor." It wouldn't be the last time.

When I was in college, I dated a girl, Emily, who invited me home to meet her parents. I'm sure they were curious to find out who this kid from Detroit was that their daughter was seeing. I drove there in my trusty 1985 Oldsmobile Cutlass Supreme, and the first thing I noticed was how big their house was. The second thing I noticed was they didn't have bars on the windows. Until that point, the only houses I'd seen without bars were on TV.

We were about to sit down to dinner when I brought a contraption into their house. It was something like an anti-theft club but with a metal bracket that goes around a car's steering wheel and ignition to prevent someone from hotwiring the car and stealing it. I locked my car and brought the whole thing inside.

Her parents were polite—"nice to meet you" kind of conversation—and while we were at the table, they asked me what the contraption was. All excited, I told them it was a club and steering column lock, so someone can't bust a car's ignition and hotwire it. "I'm going to get a detachable steering wheel," I told my girlfriend's parents, "so if anyone does bust in, they can't drive off."

Her mom looked at me and asked, "Where do you stay where you feel you need all of that?"

She wasn't looking down on me, she was genuinely curious.

I literally felt as small as an ant.

Everyone in my neighborhood had clubs and column locks. I even shaved the locks on my car doors so people couldn't break in. That was normal where I lived. It was a "cool" status symbol if you had all the high-tech, anti-theft gear.

For the first time in my life, I realized I had never thought about that. I had never thought about why I lived in a place where I felt I needed all of that.

At the dinner table, I played it off like a joke. "Oh, I'm just kidding. I just thought it would be cool to take the steering wheel off."

I felt so deflated after that question. That's when I started seriously thinking that something had to change.

## TWO JOBS ARE FOR TWO PEOPLE

Early on, I saw my mom work two jobs, but we never really got ahead. I came from a single parent household and always assumed that was what I'd have to do, too. So, in high school I got creative about how to make money and legally get around the system.

Child labor laws limit the number of hours that kids under 18 can work when school is in session, but if there was a loophole, you could trust me to find it. The laws specified that you couldn't work a full 40 hours for one employer, but my high school offered what was called a "co-op"—a student could go to school half a day and then learn a trade for the second half of the school day. And there was another option—you could find your own paid internship.

Since I was already working at a department store called Mervyn's of California, I approached the management team there, asking if I could turn my position into a paid internship—which simply meant they'd have to fill out some paperwork for the school, describing what I was learning by working this job and telling the school how I was doing as an intern. I was a good employee—I figured they'd go for it, and they did. So, every day, I left my school halfway through the day and went to my paid internship where I handled cash and learned about business instead of being in class. Then, after school, I had a second job at McDonalds at first and later at Best Buy—working evenings and weekends. Between the internship and my after-school job, I worked 40 hours a week through high school.

I thought that's what I had to do to get ahead, yet at the same time I had begun to realize that two jobs are for two people. I was sacrificing all my free time to work. I never played sports because I couldn't miss work for practice schedules and away games. Since I knew I wasn't going to the NBA anyway, I thought I'd rather work and make money—but, in trying to get ahead, I missed out on a lot during my teenage years.

I started thinking about how to get one good job so I didn't have to work two. As a high school kid, I had no idea what a "good job" was, but I wanted something with a key card. Getting to scan in and out of a building and different rooms seemed like top tier to me—all those people got to wear regular clothes to work, not some branded company polo.

I got it into my head that I would study business in college to accomplish that goal. But what did that really mean? Like a lot of people, I wanted to go to college for a generic business degree.

## "WHAT DO THEY DO" HOUSES

Emily's parents—who had asked me why I needed all that anti-theft equipment—lived in Canton, Michigan. When I saw their big, beautiful brick house with open, clear windows, I called it a "What do they do" house because, walking up to it, it made me think, "What do they do to live in a house like that?" I wanted to live in a house like that someday. I asked Emily's parents about their jobs, and they were both engineers. It was in that moment that I decided I was going to be one too.

I switched my major from business to mechanical engineering and then to electrical engineering and completed engineering courses all the way up to my senior year. But in my junior year, I began hearing that engineering graduates couldn't find jobs. "Wait," I thought, "I still have two years left to go. By the time I graduate, there will be two years' worth of engineering grads who can't find jobs." On top of that, there were a lot of other engineering schools in the state: Michigan State, University of Michigan, Lawrence Tech, Kettering, and others. I could see where this was headed.

Emily's parents were very gracious and let me go to work with them to see what engineers did. Her stepdad worked on litigation for car accidents, testifying in lawsuits from an engineering standpoint for one of the Big Three auto companies. It was interesting but not exciting. Her mom worked on a safety project where they crashed cars to test safety features in the basement of the plant, using dummies with lasers. She explained how they monitored which car parts, if any, came in contact with the dummy and how that would manifest in an injury. They tested every part of the car, what flew off, what broke, whether it hit a person, and what injuries it caused. I thought it was very, very cool. They'd send the components back with feedback to build better systems and parts for the cars.

The day they let me go to work with them at the engineering facility, we were in a basement with no windows and one of their co-workers said, "Oh yeah, Karen and Brandon and I have been on this project for fifteen or twenty years."

"Oh, you only work with each other?" I asked.

"Yeah," he replied.

I couldn't imagine working in a windowless basement with the same two people for 15 to 20 years. And that, combined with learning that engineers were not getting jobs like they used to, made me decide I didn't want to be an engineer after all.

I was back to square one, not really sure what I wanted to do with my life.

## I COULD HAVE LOST MY MONEY ON MY OWN

What first led me to the stock market was that I'd always heard it was where really wealthy people made their money. I didn't know anyone personally who was rich, but all the rich white people on TV talked about the stock market. I knew nothing about it other than that. I thought, how hard could this be? We were nearing the end of the dot-com boom where it seemed like everyone was getting rich off technology stocks and I kept thinking, "How do I get a piece?"

I was 18 years old, and I'd often heard people say if you put $2K into the stock market at this age and let it sit, you'd be a millionaire in 40 years. I didn't know why everyone didn't do that, so I decided not to be like everyone else and do it. I didn't know where to invest or how to invest, so I opened an investment account at a well-known bank. To fund my first account, I used $2,000 of my high school graduation money.

The investment advisor asked me two questions.

"Why do you want to invest?"

"To be rich," I said. "Why else would anyone want to do this?" I thought it was an obvious answer.

Her second question was, "So, you want aggressive funds, right?"

"Yeah, I'm eighteen, I want aggressive growth." That sounded like the fastest way to grow my money.

And that was that. The advisor probably got a commission for opening an account for a kid off the street, and I left the account alone to grow, thinking that I'd come back to about $6K in a few years.

Two years later I logged into my account and discovered it was down to $700! I'd thought that licensed, professional investment advisors didn't lose money, but clearly, they did. Getting to millionaire status wasn't going to be as simple as sticking money in an account and waiting 40 years.

A little confused, I went to see the woman at the bank who had invested my money and asked what happened.

"Well, the market goes up and it goes down."

"I could have lost my money on my own," I said. "I thought I'd come back to a big chunk of change and be on my way." I told her to give me my $700 and I'd invest it myself.

After closing the account, I took the remaining $700, bought a pair of $200 gym shoes to make myself feel better, and decided to take things into my own hands with the remaining $500.

At the time, I was working as a Sprint PCS cell phone sales rep inside a Best Buy store, making $8 an hour plus commission. At that point, I wasn't looking to quit my job, but I didn't want to work Saturdays anymore. All my family and friends' events, barbeques, and other get-togethers happened on the weekends, and I kept missing out on those things. So, I thought if I could make $50 a week, I could drop my Saturday shift.

With the $500 left from my graduation money, I thought—as many people do—I would invest in the company I work for. Sprint stock happened to be at $5 a share, so I bought 100 shares, thinking that if it went up 50 cents, I'd make $50—then I wouldn't have to work weekends. That was 10 cents a day for five days. I thought, "that's not asking for much."

So, I was back in the investment game, but this time I was controlling my own destiny. I would check on my stock daily, several times a day, almost obsessed with how the stock moved hour by hour. My obsession immediately was met with disappointment. As soon as I bought the stock, it started to drop. By the end of the week, I didn't make $50—I was down roughly $100 as the stock fell from $5 a share to $4 a share.

I remembered hearing, "You have to be in it for the long run," so I tried not to panic. In another week's time the stock had made its way back to $5 a share and I was at break-even. At that point I thought, "Okay, go to five dollars and fifty cents a share so I can make my fifty dollars." Once again, the stock fell to $4 by the end of the week.

I was pissed off and frustrated, believing the stock market was rigged. I was convinced it was a game of luck and there was no rhyme or reason to the whole investing thing.

The following week the stock made its way back up to $5 a share, but this time I decided to get out of the stock at $5 a share which was my break-even. Then I watched the stock fall back down to $4 a share and bought 100 shares again. As the stock moved back up to $5 a share, I sold my shares and made my first $100 in the stock market.

Making my first $100 profit proved to me that I could make the stock market work for me by following predictable, repeatable patterns. Later, I'd call this type of stock movement "one of the three most profitable patterns." I began to wonder what other patterns exist, how to find them, and how to make money off them. For the next several months, I spent countless hours studying stocks, researching patterns, and learning that certain patterns show up over and over again. By recognizing these patterns, you can—with a certain amount of accuracy—predict where a stock is headed.

I got really good at making hundreds of dollars off my original $500, but this would not get me rich. Yes, you heard me right—I had moved on from wanting to make $50 and was now ready to go after riches. Most of the other stocks I found that repeated the patterns I'd seen were too expensive for my trading account size, and I began to ask myself how I could get more money into my account.

Around this time, two of my cousins went to an investment seminar—you know, the kind that they hold in a hotel ballroom. They learned about options. I had no idea what options were and how crucial a role they would later play in my success. All I knew is that my cousins were excited. One of them told me, "Jay, I think we found it, I think we found the key to really taking advantage of the investment game." The other cousin, although excited, only saw the risk and decided to take his shot at building wealth through network marketing. I asked them if I could look over and study the material they'd brought home from the seminar.

By using options, I learned I had a way to invest in or trade the higher price stocks that were initially out of our reach by controlling the stocks instead of owning them. This was a game changer because I had found patterns like those I'd seen with Sprint in higher priced stocks. Up to this point, all I could do was watch from the sidelines because these stocks were anywhere from $100 to $2,000 a share, but now I had a way to capitalize on them. After learning about call and put options—I'll explain about those in the chapters ahead—and scaling my original $500 account up with better returns by controlling the stock—as opposed to buying and owning the stock directly—I looked into how I could get more money into "the machine," aka the stock market.

I was on an academic scholarship to Wayne State University's Mike Ilitch School of Business, and I had seen others get student loan refund checks and use them for rent, shopping, partying, whatever. I learned that if I applied for student loans, my scholarship would cover my tuition and the student loan would come back to me as a refund. So, I applied and received a $10K student loan refund check that I planned to use to invest in the stock market.

Now, I know you may be thinking, "But isn't that risky?" The short answer is no. The way I looked at it was that I was already making money with the small account I had, so I would be doing the same thing with a little more money and getting a bigger result. I also analyzed the risk of losing the student loan money. It had 0% to low interest that did not start accumulating until after graduation. That meant that I had four years to invest that money and—if I lost it—I had four years to earn it back to pay back the government. I also realized that even if it took me longer than four years, I would be like everybody else who had student loans making small monthly payments—but if I was right and could grow this $10K, I would be rich. It was an easy calculated risk to take.

What I could not ignore was the thought of making more money in the stock market. If I was right about using the student loan to do what I was already doing with a smaller amount, I would eventually be in a situation where I would never have to worry about money again.

When I look back, this was one of the defining moments of my life—learning how to calculate risk versus reward and how to take a calculated risk to carve out my own path instead of being afraid of doing what others thought was risky.

I took that $10K student loan and grew it to $113K in under a year as a 21-year-old college student.

My cousin was also doing well in the stock market. We couldn't believe that we were on a path to making more money than our parents were making working 40 to 60 hours a week, and we were doing it without working hard for the money. Our money was working hard for us in the stock market.

As we started making engineer-, lawyer-, doctor-type money, we moved into our separate condo apartments and decided it was time to level up and enjoy some of the finer things in life. My cousin got his brand-new Cadillac Escalade and paid for it in cash, which eventually led me to getting my new Lexus and customizing it with 20-inch rims.

## WE DON'T DRIVE DURING RUSH HOUR

Our lifestyle started to change drastically. My cousin and I quit our jobs and felt like we could literally print money from the stock market. We would meet every day at his apartment or mine to have breakfast and go over stocks. I remember my neighbors thinking that, in addition to the Lexus, I owned a Cadillac Escalade because my cousin was at my place so often.

When the stock market closed at 4 p.m., we would relax, play video games, take a nap, or go to happy hour until rush hour died down. We used to joke that we don't drive during rush hour—that's for people who have jobs.

We were spending money left and right because we felt like we could always print some more. I went into Best Buy and bought the most custom sound system with pure glass speakers. I had a cherry bark-oak sleigh bed and granite tops on my dresser and nightstands. Everything I had was nice, not gaudy—it was classy. But, ironically, as much as we'd wanted so passionately to get out of the old neighborhood, my cousin and I never spent any money on going anywhere special. We spent a lot of money on living high-end in Metro Detroit, but we didn't travel and see the world. Our focus was on living the high life locally.

Money became almost a joke to us. I remember hitting a pothole and cracking one of the expensive rims on my Lexus and thinking, "Man, I gotta spend another eight hundred on one rim, ha-ha-ha." That actually happened twice—I bent two rims and had to spend $800 on each, but with the money we were making it really felt like no big deal.

I was living the life: money, cars, girls, nice apartment, no job, controlled my own clock, no driving during rush hour. What more could you ask for? Everyone in our circle grew to respect my cousin and me. We had a life people admired and one some probably even envied. Strangers would often ask us what we were doing for a living, and we'd tell them we're investors.

When we were out with my cousin's dad, he would introduce us to people, saying, "Oh yeah, they're into stocks." You could tell he was really proud of us.

For three years in a row, we'd made $100K a year and assumed it could only get better from there. I thought, "Where are we going to be in five years or ten years? We're going to be so rich we'll be throwing money out the window!"

It never occurred to us that we could lose all our money. We'd lost small amounts before, like a couple grand, and then we would make $10K or $20K back.

The skill of making money on stocks came easy to us. The more confident we became, the more risks we took. Eventually, we stopped doing the early morning research. By the time year four rolled around, we weren't meeting as regularly—and when we did meet, we'd ask if we were doing research and then kind of blow it off. "Did you do your research?"

"Nah, but that stock's fine."

We started letting things slide. We were getting cocky.

We had separate investment accounts, but we always talked about our trades—what do we think about this company's stock, what's our upside, what's our downside, what news did we find on the stock, when is this company reporting earnings, and do we think the company is going to miss or beat its earnings and profit numbers … how will the stock behave after earnings? We'd always shared our thoughts.

Looking back, there was one trade that seemed like a turning point. I asked my cousin if he got into that trade and he said, "Eh, yeah, a little." I gave the same response when he asked me. That one trade was the first time we weren't completely open and honest about how much we put in and how much we both lost. And that was the one trade where we both lost a lot of money. It was the beginning of when we started to hide our losses from each other. We stopped talking about the market as much and started doing things privately.

My cousin realized he needed to diversify and got into real estate, but he didn't tell me that until much later. It felt like a betrayal to our joint success after we had collaborated in the stock market so closely for three years.

In that one trade where we weren't completely open and honest, my cousin bought double the shares. When he finally told me, I bought triple to "one up" him and the stock went against us. We both lost big on that one.

It got to the point where if we lost money in a trade, we'd downplay it and say, "Eh, I only lost a little."

I'm not sure if it was ego—not wanting him to make more than I did—or cockiness—assuming we couldn't lose any money—or a combination of both, but that was the beginning of the end. Up until that point, I thought we were untouchable. I never thought I'd end up flat broke.

**CHAPTER 1: TAKEAWAYS**

- You must expand your environment to think bigger.
- Always look for the loopholes in life.
- Just because someone went to school for finance or has a license to invest doesn't mean they can't lose money.
- Understand how to calculate real risk versus reward.
- Never stop doing the foundational work it takes to be successful.

CHAPTER 2

# Down But Not Out

I realized something important about my early rise and fall in the stock market years later. The trouble started the day my cousin and I stopped doing the research. We stopped doing what made us successful in the first place. Those little slips started adding up, just as they do with a diet. No one says, "Oh, I think I'll be obese." They start out with a slip, "I'm going to have an extra candy bar today." Then another slip, "I should work out today, but I had a rough day at work. I'll do it tomorrow." That rough day becomes a rough week and so on. People don't see these little slips building up.

When we were making money hand over fist, I thought, "We don't need to do our research today," or, "If we're losing money, let's double down. We'll make it back." That was a gambler's mentality. We slowly slipped away from the careful research and methodical planning that brought us success. It wasn't until my second big loss that I realized I was in trouble financially. In all, I lost roughly 250K, but it didn't happen all at once.

When I lost a chunk of money, I'd immediately turn around and do another trade, which I call revenge trading. This is where you ignore all logic, research, and technical analysis and forget your personal game plan. You're focused solely on getting your money back, regardless of if it's a good trade or not. That was me. I wanted to get my money back. When I would revenge trade, a $75K loss would quickly turn into another $50K loss for a total of $125K.

From there, it kept getting worse and worse. I wasn't losing it all at once, but I was losing it in large chunks, and it turned into gambling—or shall I say I turned into a gambler. I eventually realized that it wasn't going to end well, but it was too late.

There's a mathematical formula to calculate the percentage gain you need to recover from a loss and break even. That formula is Percentage Gain Needed = (Loss Percentage / (100 - Loss Percentage) x 100)

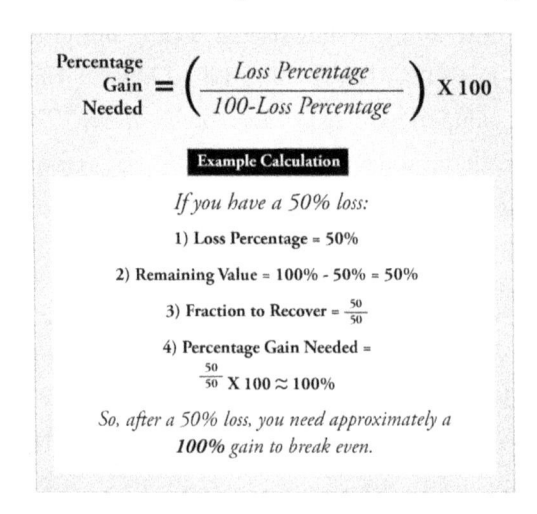

$$\text{Percentage Gain Needed} = \left( \frac{\text{Loss Percentage}}{100 - \text{Loss Percentage}} \right) \times 100$$

**Example Calculation**

*If you have a 50% loss:*

1) Loss Percentage = 50%

2) Remaining Value = 100% - 50% = 50%

3) Fraction to Recover = $\frac{50}{50}$

4) Percentage Gain Needed =
$\frac{50}{50}$ X 100 ≈ 100%

*So, after a 50% loss, you need approximately a* ***100%*** *gain to break even.*

Mathematically if you lose 50%, you must make 100% to get it back. If you lose 75% you need to make 300% to get it all back.

If your next trade hinges on making 300% or more, it's ridiculous to think you can wake up and quickly find a 300% trade when your last few trades were losers of 50% or more.

I was cocky, assuming I was going to hit 50% to 100%+ home runs in the stock market, especially considering I'd stopped doing what it took to be successful in this industry. I could have quit or at least taken a break to regroup with the $125K I had left. I would have been okay for another year or so until I figured out what I was doing wrong, took a step back, and traded smaller or not at all. I had no bills that equaled a quarter-million dollars. I only needed about $3K a month to pay my costs of living. I was mostly living a debt-free life.

The most ironic part was that I didn't really need the money I was chasing after in the stock market. I could have slowed down and re-grouped when I took my first big loss. But *nooo*! All I could think was that I wanted my money back in the next trade regardless of whether it was a good trade or not. My mindset was that the market was holding onto "my" money, and I wanted it back *now*. I never stopped to ask myself, "Why do you need the money back? Why do you need it back so quickly?"

The more I lost, the more I revenge traded, my confidence diminished and, well, living the high life didn't last very long, although the memories will last forever.

## TIME TO PREPARE FOR GOING BROKE

I could see the outcome. My account was not headed in the right direction. I was bleeding cash, and it was only a matter of time before I went broke. The first thing I did was make a spreadsheet of every bill and every dollar I had coming in and going out. I knew my financial situation down to the exact day—I had 4 months and 16 days before I ran out of money. I wasn't making the money back fast enough, so I started to do damage control. I put my Lexus up for sale. It took me three months and two weeks to sell it, two weeks before I would miss my first car payment. I sold it before my credit would take a negative hit for multiple missed payments, which would have ultimately led to the car to being repossessed. I put in my notice at my apartment, so I didn't have an eviction on my record. I was super proactive, all the while watching my accounts deflate from multiple six figures down to zero.

Although I was super aware of what was happening, I was still in denial—or maybe I was in shock. It took me at least three months to admit I needed a job. I kept asking myself, "Do I need a job? Do I want a job? I need one, but I don't want one."

I had previously joined a network marketing company and decided I was going to use those three remaining months to build a second stream of income in that industry. The only problem was, my real money had been coming from the stock market, not the network marketing business. I'd already been in it for two years before going broke from the stock market. The reality was, if I hadn't made any money in network marketing during those two years, what was going to change in the next three months?

I received checks for a few grand from the stock market and the network marketing group that prolonged the inevitable, but I ultimately had to face the reality that I wasn't going to make the money back quickly. I was forced to move back in with my mom and get a job.

Since I'd cut off my internet, I spent a lot of time at Panera Bread, taking advantage of their free Wi-Fi. I was so broke, there were times when their free bread samples were my only meal for the day. I'd go to Panera dressed in a suit and fill out job applications on my laptop—I looked like a businessman, but I was searching for jobs and getting free food. It was one of the lowest points of my life.

I downplayed how bad it was, telling people "I'm thinking about moving back to my childhood home to prepare for my next big opportunity," as if I had some huge business deal I was working on. The truth was, I was broke and technically homeless. On the outside it looked like I was busy, but I was dying on the inside and really praying someone would hire me.

Putting on the nice suit was for my dignity. I looked good in a suit. I wanted to dress for success. My bank accounts were drained, my credit cards maxed out—but that wasn't visible. My outward appearance was all that remained. Without the suit, someone would know that something had changed and that I was not doing well financially—or mentally for that matter.

I could have done other things—like finding a roommate to help cut costs—but short-term solutions were not the answer. I needed drastic change, not help with the bills. "No," I thought, "I gotta rebuild." Rebuilding would require significant changes and sacrifice, not some temporary band-aid solution. So, I did what I had to do, no matter how tough. I moved back home but felt defeated.

Some people, when they get into financial trouble, worry about what other people think. Then they prolong making the inevitable sacrifices until they're forced to, and they end up hurting themselves for a lot longer. They do things like hold onto the car until it gets repossessed rather than be proactive. I didn't need to bandage my wounds, I needed to perform open-heart surgery on my entire life. I was willing to let it go to stop the bleeding and eventually come back even stronger.

Somehow my cousin didn't end up in the same situation, at least not immediately. I've always felt that when the two of us stopped talking about our investments, it drove a wedge between us. When I told him I was broke and had to move back home he said, "Oh, I'm on my fifth unit."

"Fifth unit, what is that?"

He was secretly buying real estate and hadn't told me.

"Hello, were you going to tell your business partner?" I'd thought of us as business partners. Even though we had separate accounts and made our own decisions, we'd always shared the opportunity and the research … at least we had in the past.

For the first time in my life, I said to myself, "I gotta look out for me." Up until then I thought I was looking out for "we." I honestly felt betrayed.

When I moved home, my mom was happy to help me out and let me live rent free. She was happy to have her son home, but I barely spent time there. It was just a place to lay my head because I was so focused on getting out of debt and supporting myself again. I worked every extra hour I could. Whenever someone needed to stay late or come in early at my job, I volunteered. When they needed people on holidays, I signed up. And when I wasn't working, I would study until late at night at Starbucks.

I kept telling myself that it was temporary. "Oh, I'm not moving back home. I'm putting my stuff there temporarily while I find my next place." And through it all, I kept up a super positive mindset, even when being positive didn't change anything.

I ended up staying at my mom's for about a year before I started working my way out of debt and was able to support myself again. While I was living there, I didn't buy extravagant stuff, but I was paying for food, my cell phone, and going on dates. I still had my 1985 Cutlass and was paying to keep that thing running. I did spend some money to keep up the appearance that I was doing well. It was all going on credit cards because that was the only way to avoid being cut off from my old lifestyle completely. The thing is, when the bottom falls out of your life, you don't think, "Oh, I'm broke," and then scale back 100%. When you go out to eat, you still want that steak. When someone asks if you want to go on vacation in Florida, you say, "Yeah, sure, let's go." You don't say, "Hey, not sure if you know this but I'm flat broke."

My last trip to Florida was with my cousin and best friend. We partied, dined out, and rented jet skis. Whatever the total came to for that trip, it was the last charge on my credit card before it was maxed out. My mindset was, "This is it. I'm going to default on my credit cards anyway. I might as well have fun before things get really bad." So, I went to Florida as a kind of "last hurrah." Not spending that last money on my credit card wasn't going to save me, anyway.

Some good advice: if you find yourself in a hole, stop digging. In my mind, the banks were going to add interest and late fees to my remaining available credit. That money was going to get eaten up one way or another if I didn't spend it. I chose to throw myself a farewell party before it got really bad.

## HOW MY DEBT REALLY SPIRALED OUT OF CONTROL

The creditors began calling me and I went through three stages of denial. At first, I thought, "I don't want to ruin my credit." Then I went through a phase thinking, "Well, before my credit is completely ruined, let's negotiate." Then, finally, I arrived at, "Well, I'm not paying anyone because it won't matter anyway." I didn't own anything they could repossess so I didn't care.

I told creditors to call me when they were ready to write it off or give me a 50% discount.

Then it became, "Oh, I owe you ten thousand dollars? Call me when you're ready to take three thousand."

If they could come down to $3K, I'd pay it off quickly with my commission checks. But if they wanted the full $10K, I'd be paying them for what felt like the rest of my life. They wouldn't take the $3K, so I hung up—because what were they going to do? I didn't have a house or assets they could seize. There was nothing for them to take. Repossess my car? I'd already sold the Lexus.

For me, that was the start of taking my power back. It evolved over the course of six to 12 months.

I finally had a job, but I was still in debt. I had to work two weeks before getting a paycheck. My cell phone was cut off and I was in survival mode. I had to get the phone turned back on and pay for basic necessities, like gas and groceries. Even though my mom had a room for me to stay in, I was still on my own for covering my basic costs of living. So, I wasn't thinking about credit cards.

Once the late payments hit, it was on my credit report. When the creditors called, asking if I cared about my credit report, I realized it didn't matter what I told them. They didn't have the power to remove negative marks from my credit report. I was still trying to buy groceries and pay for my phone. The damage was done.

I could take my $2K check and give Visa $300, Mastercard $400, and Discover $500. After that, I was left with $800 for cell phone, food, and gas. It left no money for rent, other living expenses, or fun. So, I decided to focus on what I needed to survive and told the creditors, "Y'all can do what you want to do to my credit report." I told myself, "Do what you have to do now to get out of this situation because negative credit marks fall off in seven years anyway. You want to make sure in seven years, you're never in this situation again." I was thinking long term, not about satisfying some credit collector in a call center somewhere.

Remember when I told you I took a $10K student loan and turned it into $113K? That loan was low interest, so I thought, "I can wait to pay that back." I wanted the money to stay invested. But I dropped out of school, so interest started accruing from that moment. Three years of interest and deferments can add up. I added them to the list of debts I most likely couldn't pay back for seven years.

What hurt me the most was that when I was making $100K a year for those three years in the stock market, I never paid any taxes. I got bad tax advice and was told I didn't have to pay taxes on anything for three years and that I would be able to write off a lot of things.

What I misunderstood was that the IRS doesn't come after you for unpaid taxes for three years. I thought I didn't have to pay them for three years. After three years of not paying taxes and making $100K a year, I owed $75K in taxes plus penalties and interest. Between the IRS, student loans, and credit cards, I was in extreme debt.

I had hit the final level of poor credit when I had a tax lien slapped on my credit report from the federal government. I told the people from the credit card company to get in line behind the IRS. That was a turning point. They weren't going to get their money ahead of the IRS. They started to settle to get what they could. For example, they took that $3K instead of the $10K I originally owed. Not having any access to credit was a blessing in disguise because all it did was force me to learn to live off cash.

I needed a good-paying job, but I had to think strategically. Since it was going to take me at least five years to pay all these people, I decided it would be smart to go back to school and earn a degree. It would increase my value to a company. To do this I wanted a job that had tuition reimbursement.

I figured if I could get a commission sales job with descent base pay, I could live off the hourly rate but hustle to get big commission checks. Then I could use my commission to pay off debt faster and get back into the stock market game. I went back to the only thing I had a background in—selling cell phones, this time with Verizon Wireless.

Verizon checked all the boxes for me—plus, if I could get a discount on something I had to pay for anyway, like a cell phone, it would allow me to keep more money in my pocket to get out of debt faster and back to investing.

The government was keeping all my tax returns, and I wouldn't get a refund, but that would pay down the tax debt I owed.

I might have been down, but I was definitely not out.

## A PHOENIX RISING FROM THE ASHES

After doing the math, it was clear it would take me what felt like the rest of my life to pay back all my debts. If I didn't get back into the stock market, all I would be left with was working hard to pay them a good chunk of my paycheck every month. Every time I worked overtime or sold more phones, the government—through taxes and my tax lien—as well as my creditors would say, "Thank you for working hard, pay me and get back to work." If I continued doing what I was doing, I'd be trapped by my debt and owned by the credit card companies for years to come.

I started to ask, "How can I pay this back faster and get back to being free?" If I paid above the minimum required to pay things off faster, I'd be paying them until I was 50. If I paid the minimum, I could then take the difference and invest in the market and possibly be done with paying off all my debt in roughly five years. There was no cap on how much I could make or how quickly I could make it from the stock market. I wanted back into the game.

Part of my five-year plan was to earn my degree. During that time, five years of tax returns would be paid toward back taxes. I'd live off my hourly wage and use my commission checks and bonuses to invest in the stock market. By the time I graduated, I'd make enough through the market to pay everyone off. In the meantime, I'd pay things down little by little so I wouldn't owe as much.

I went back to school to get a degree in finance. After having previous success in the stock market, I was passionate about finance. I also thought I needed to raise my floor. You see, when I went flat broke, the only job I could get was working in the mall selling phones again. I'm not knocking anyone who works in the mall or sells cell phones, but every job I looked at that paid $80K to $100K required a degree. I told myself that if I ever got knocked down in life again, I need my financial floor to be $80K- to $100K-type jobs. I would need to qualify for jobs in that salary range as opposed to a $40K base salary. After making $100,000 in the stock market, going back down to a $40K base was like falling through the floor and climbing back up out of the basement. So, with a degree in hand I would essentially raise my floor.

Although I initially avoided my creditors, knowing they couldn't do much to me because of the federal government's tax lien, I decided to call the IRS and talk to them about the situation because I knew they had the power to garnish my wages. I was glad I did. They weren't nearly as scary as people make them out to be. In fact, my revenue-collection officer informed me of a one-time forgiveness plan if you've never been in trouble with the IRS before—they would essentially cut a chunk of the interest and fees as well as set up a payment plan.

With this news I was motivated to sell as many phones as I could to get bigger commission checks. I was even more motivated to get back into the stock market because paying the IRS back seemed so much more doable now and within my five-year time frame.

So, I was in grind mode—all I wanted to do was work on my debt repayment plan and crush my commission sales goals. I started hitting $7K commission checks, which I was investing and getting good returns on. I was paying the IRS tax lien down and was back in school, so I didn't have to pay my student loans back immediately. I deferred them again, which meant I had more money to invest or pay down debt and negotiate better settlements, whichever I chose.

After about a year, I got to a point where I was completely out of consumer debt except for my student loans, and after roughly three years I had paid the IRS back and my tax lien was released. Initially, I didn't make extra payments to the IRS. I didn't need my credit for anything. I already had a used car, I had an apartment again, and I had learned to live below my means and pay cash for everything. Side note: I was surprised I was able to get an apartment with a tax lien, but when they looked at my income to expense ratio, even with the tax payments I could afford the apartment.

Year five, I graduated with a bachelor's degree. My student loans could be deferred to maybe six months after graduation and then payments would start again. There was nowhere to hide. I remember the student loan repayment office calling and saying it was time to make payments. They had a "no questions asked" hardship policy, so I continued to tell them I was still in financial hardship, and they said they would defer my payments again. I used that maybe twice to buy me more time, then the loan officer said, "Okay, in order to defer again you have to send us your bank statements." They would see that I was not in hardship, and it was time to start allocating money to those student loan debts.

After resuming student loan payments, I found a Jaguar I wanted to buy and even got approved for it. Before then, I'd never looked at my student loan statement. One night I prayed and said, "God am I ready? Is this it? Can I get back into a luxury car? All my debts are paid off except for my student loans." I heard a voice, not an audible one, but it was like God spoke to me and said, "Go look at your student loan document." I got out of bed in the middle of the night and looked. At the time, I was paying about $1,600 a month for student loans. I wasn't that worried because I was making money again and most of my debt had been paid off.

However, when I looked at my statement it recorded that I'd made a $1,600 payment, but $800 of that was going to interest. Half of my payment wasn't even paying down the principle on the loans!

I felt sick to my stomach knowing that roughly $800 was going up in smoke every single month. I'm a numbers guy, and I thought if I get this Jaguar with roughly an $800 monthly payment, it would really be a $1,600 monthly payment because that would be money I'm not using to pay down the student loan. I'd throw $800 a month away in interest even longer because it would take me longer to pay it back now that I have a car note.

"Okay, let's go to work," I told myself. "You can get this car but only as a reward for paying off your student loans." I buckled down and paid it all off maybe six months later.

If I paid off the loan and didn't get the car, I'd have $2,400 free a month after the loan was paid off. This is why understanding numbers and math is important. You see, once I paid the loan off, it would free up $1,600 a month, but $800 was going up in smoke to interest. So,

$1,600 a month payment back in my pocket with $800 of it now available to go toward something real and tangible instead of interest would be worth $2,400 to me in real value.

I worked hard, paid everything off, and then got myself the car as a reward. I even recorded when they delivered the car to me on my YouTube channel.

That was the last of my debt, I was finally free again.

## DOWN BUT NOT OUT

A lot of people, when they experience large financial losses from investing, feel scared or hesitant about getting back into the stock market. Not me. I knew how the stock market worked and had tasted success. I was determined to figure out how to profit from the market again and figure out what I did wrong so I could come back bigger, stronger, and more knowledgeable than ever before. That's where all my investment principles come from—principles I'll share with you throughout this book.

I was never nervous about getting back in, but I did approach investing differently. I was planning for "not so sunny day" scenarios. Although I was out of debt and back into investing, I was more cautious because I could never forget the pain I felt from losing it all.

There were three key things that got me through those difficult years: knowing the numbers, having a game plan, and having a personal development plan. If you have debt, once you know the numbers, there's power in knowing exactly how long it's going to take to pay it off if you don't do anything different. You can accept that, or you can start to strategize from your worst-case scenario and look for ways to speed up paying everything back. For me, the way to speed things up was through commission sales and investing. Know where your money is going—like when I discovered that 50% of my student loan payments were going to interest and not to paying back the loan. When you know the numbers, you can plan to get a better job and keep your standard of living low while paying down your debts. Or you can temporarily reduce your standard of living and put more toward paying down your debts.

So, if you're in debt, grab a pencil and piece of paper or a spreadsheet like I did. Write down how much you owe and who you owe it to. It's a good idea to write down interest rates and the amount of time it will take to pay off debts with minimum payments. Write down your income and living expenses separate from your debt. You can then start to look at where you can trim your expenses or options for increasing your income if necessary. It's a basic first step to taking control of your financial situation.

## KNOW THE NUMBERS

When I looked at the spreadsheet that tracked my income versus my debt, I realized I could get a better job and pay my debt off in 20 years instead of 40. But if I invested, I could pay it off in five years. This is the power of knowing the numbers and having a game plan. You can only have a strategic game plan if you face your debt head on and don't ignore it as if it's going to magically go away.

I also read and listened to a lot of self-improvement and personal development books to help with my mindset. It was still a dark time for me, trying to dig out of that hole. Even with my game plan, it was a low point in my life.

Entrepreneur and author Jim Rohn's personal development seminar, "How to Have Your Best Year Ever," talks about how he kept a list of people who had negatively impacted his life on his "payback" list—like the credit card company.[1] Once they were paid, he'd never owe them money again. My personal payback list included Discover, Mastercard, the IRS, and a few others.

I'd begun journaling and recording everything going on in my life. I'd heard Jim Rohn say in his seminar that it's important to document everything and take pictures, because one day you'd look back at this moment that you thought was the worst time of your life and realize it was what made you. If anyone ever asks, "How did you do it, how did you climb from the bottom to the top?" your personal journal and wisdom will be worth millions.

That helped give me the idea of starting my YouTube channel, *The Brown Report,* and documenting everything about my climb out of the bottom of the financial pit. I documented when I moved back home. I documented selling my personal belongings. I documented getting back into the stock market. And I documented eventually becoming a millionaire.

---

[1] "Jim Rohn: How to Have Your Best Year Ever! Seminar | Full Transcript," Spread Great Ideas, accessed May 5, 2024, https://spreadgreatideas.org/resources/speeches/jim-rohn-how-to-have-your-best-year-ever-seminar-full-transcript/.

**CHAPTER 2: TAKEAWAYS**

- Revenge trading will make you abort all logic and have you ignoring dangerous red flags.
- If you find yourself in a financial hole, stop digging.
- Everyone needs to understand how taxes work.
- Get a job that aligns with helping you achieve your goals.
- Know the true cost of debt and financing.

CHAPTER 3

# Power Charts, Power Trades, Power Profits

**When bad things happened to** me—or at least what I perceived to be bad things in the moment—I had a tendency to ask why was it happening to me. What did I do wrong? I played the blame Game.

After time passed, I saw that bad things didn't happen *to* me, they happened *for* me. If I hadn't lost all that money, if I didn't have to move back in with my mom, I would never have been able to help millions of people with my YouTube channel. I would never have known how strong I was if I hadn't come back from a place where I was broke and broken. Although it took me a while to get back to and eventually pass my previous level of success, if I had never gone through the trials and tribulations, I would not be as strong a person in character and in my trading principles as I am today.

When I did return to the stock market using my new-found trading principles, I came back to experiencing a new level of success. On the second day of the year—January 2, 2020—I made 100K in one day. (The market was closed on January 1 because it was New Year's Day.) It was hard to believe that in one day I had made what would have taken me all year to make working 40 to 50 hours a week.

Maybe you're currently trading and not hitting the levels of success you believe you should be, or you're brand new to the industry and looking to get into the game. You might be thinking, "I could never do big numbers like that."

We all have to start somewhere, and most of us wonder what's possible. We've all seen people post huge profit numbers on social media and wonder if it's even real. We wonder if it can be duplicated and, if so, we wonder if and how we can do something similar in the stock market.

I initially started with $500 and trying to make $50 a week so I wouldn't have to work weekends selling cell phones for Sprint PCS. I didn't wake up and say, "Oh, I'm going to make $100K in one day." Continue to hone your trading skills by spotting profitable patterns and get good at learning how to take low-risk, high-reward trades that pay off. As you do, your belief in what's possible will grow as you realize it's all a game of math and numbers. $100K days are inevitable with the right trade and amount of power behind the trade—power means owning a lot of shares or controlling a considerable amount of stock shares using options.

As I reflect back, the best part about the whole $100K trade was that the stock didn't make a big move. It was only a $2 move, but because I had so many call option contracts controlling a large amount of stock, the payout was equivalent to what I used to have to work all year for. I was able to make the right move by reading the stock chart, spotting the pattern, and then taking advantage of it.

The ticker symbol of the company I placed the trade on is ENPH (Enphase Energy). It was a company I'd been watching for a while and one that I had discussed online with the members of my Power Trades University. ENPH is a company involved in energy storage. The pattern I saw potentially starting to form is called a "cup and handle pattern." If you can start to see where the pattern is forming, you have a pretty good idea of when to enter and exit a trade as well as when to use call or put options to supercharge your potential profit while taking on minimal risk.

When I saw the pattern forming, I bought 500 call option contracts for the $22.50 strike price.

ENPH's stock eventually rose to $300 a share in August of 2022.[2] If I'd had long-term leap options, I'd be a bazillionaire by now, but that's not part of the game—at least not how I play it. There was no way to know with absolute certainty that the stock would eventually go that high. Trading is about taking advantage of short-term pattern and price movement and being happy when you pull in 50% or 100% in 30 days or less while most people are getting 7% to 10% returns a year.

When you recognize a pattern in the chart that's repeated in the

---

2 "Enphase Energy, Inc. (ENPH)," Yahoo! Finance, accessed July 10, 2024, https://finance.yahoo.com/quote/ENPH/history/?period1=1659312000&period2=1661904000.

same or other stocks that lead to big moves, it stands out—it's very apparent when you see it again. Being a disciplined power trader is all about taking a low-risk, high-reward, high-probability trade on what's most likely to happen next. I took advantage of it and closed my trade out in one day. I have seen other people—and have personally experienced—watching a stock and my profits go up real high and then come down. I wasn't going to let that happen again. I chose to master one of the most powerful emotions that chew up many traders and spit them out—greed.

With 500 call option contracts, all I needed was a $2 move to make $100K. One contract controls 100 shares, so I was controlling 50,000 shares through options which I will explain in more detail later. This is the difference between controlling stocks and buying and owning stocks. If I bought 50,000 shares at $22.50 a share it would cost $1.1 million. The contracts I had only cost me $4 a contract or $200K in total, so I made that $100K by putting up $200K. This gave me a 50% return, whereas buying the stock would have produced an 8.88% return and I would have had to put up $1.1 million to make that return. In case you're thinking, "Well, good for you, but I don't have $200K to trade in the stock market," it's important to point out that the return is the return, whatever your investment might be. Even if you had $2K you would have made $1,000 profit—a 50% return.

Once you understand what you're looking for in those high-probability patterns, you can spend most of your time looking for them and then deciding if you want to take a calculated risk on a trade. After you do that, you can decide to risk "X" amount because it's a high-probability setup.

The stock on my $100K profit trade went from $26.37 to $29.35.

It moved about $3 that day. The portion I needed was only $2, so I wasn't trying to be greedy. I didn't want to repeat what happened last time. Back then, $100K profit wasn't enough for me and eventually I lost a quarter of a million dollars, leaving me flat broke. This time around, my principles told me to take the money and run. It's good money. People work a whole year for that kind of money.

**Principle: study the chart, see the pattern, and put a lot of power behind it.**

I was so excited that day, I asked the babysitter to bring my daughter into my office. I wanted her in the video as we documented—live—my making of $100K in one day. I wanted my daughter to have the memory available in the future so if anyone ever said that something is impossible—or "that's for other people"—she would remember that anything's possible in life, regardless of what other people say or think.

One day the world may tell her that this doesn't happen to regular people. She has video proof that it's possible for her dad and for her too.

## PROFITABLE CHART PATTERNS

There are many patterns in the stock market that show up in stock charts that can help you decide when to take low-risk, high-reward trades. I have found three patterns that are the most profitable to trade, relatively easy to spot, and that show up over and over again. They are **uptrending channeling**, **sideways channeling**, and **downtrending channeling**.

**Uptrending channeling** is when a stock goes up and hits a point of resistance, where the market or stock traders believe it is overvalued. It sells back down to a support limit, where stock traders think, "At this price it's a good deal or it's under-valued."

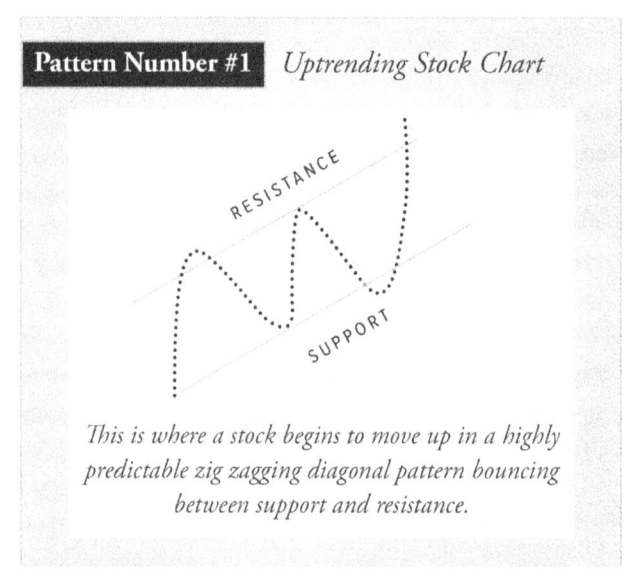

> **Pattern Number #1** *Uptrending Stock Chart*
>
> *This is where a stock begins to move up in a highly predictable zig zagging diagonal pattern bouncing between support and resistance.*

The overall trend of the stock slowly climbs even while it's hitting resistance and going back to support, making it an uptrend.

The key skill is to be able to look at a stock chart, draw the lines to determine where support and resistance are, and determine if there are predictable, repeatable patterns. If there are, then you want to sell at resistance and buy at support for the biggest profits. The stock in this pattern moves almost perfectly between the two lines in the channel. It's important to note that support and resistance define an area, not a specific number—the stock can go above or below the lines drawn on the chart.

How often does that actually happen? When you study the charts and learn what to look for, you'll realize it happens fairly often.

A pattern takes at least two points and two revolutions to form. To determine the channeling lines, a stock has to go through two resistance and two support fluctuations to make it a pattern. You've got to be ready to take action after the two points have hit and the pattern becomes clear.

Now let *me* be clear—no pattern provides a 100% guarantee that a stock is going to do what it did in the past. It's about having a 70% to 80%+ probability for what the stock is going to do next. Sometimes the pattern may look like it's forming and the stock does the opposite, which is why you must have what I like to call my "I'm Wrong Level"—a level where you risk $1 to make $3 and if you're wrong, you take that small $1 loss because the stock didn't behave in that predictable, repeatable pattern.

The second pattern is **sideways channeling**. The stock is not going up and it's not going down overall. It's channeling sideways between two support and resistance price points.

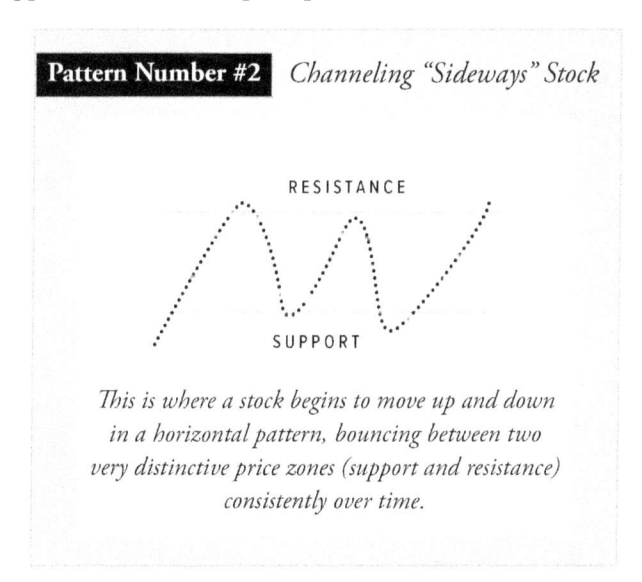

**Pattern Number #2** *Channeling "Sideways" Stock*

RESISTANCE

SUPPORT

*This is where a stock begins to move up and down in a horizontal pattern, bouncing between two very distinctive price zones (support and resistance) consistently over time.*

With a sideways channel, the pattern isn't so much about exact numbers in the rise and fall of points. It's more about an area on the chart that encompasses the pattern of the stock rising to resistance, falling back down to support, and then rising to resistance again.

By taking advantage of a sideways channel, you can still make money off a stock that isn't increasing in value over time by buying at support and selling at resistance. You can repeat the buying and selling until the stock leaves the channel and starts to form a new pattern. For instance, the stock can break out to the upside, starting an uptrend, or the stock can fall out of the bottom, starting a new downtrend. There are ways to spot the ending and beginning of a new trend, but for now it's important to recognize the three most profitable patterns when you see them.

Many people think that if they invest a huge chunk of money in one stock, 40 years later it will be worth thousands more. Unfortunately, some stocks don't increase in value that much over long periods of time. Strategically entering and exiting at support and resistance on a stock that is in a sideways channel is the way to take advantage of those stocks and profit off them in the short to medium term.

The third most profitable pattern is **downtrending channeling**. This is when you see stocks moving between two points in a channel, but the prices of support and resistance levels are trending lower, causing the channel to slope downward.

**Pattern Number #3** *Downtrending Stock Chart*

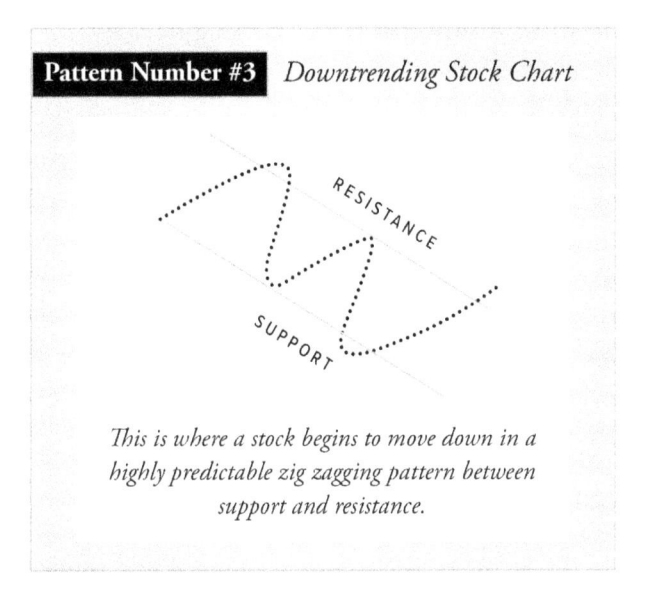

*This is where a stock begins to move down in a highly predictable zig zagging pattern between support and resistance.*

Even in a downward channel where prices are decreasing on a stock, you can still see where you could be buying and selling stock—or you could use call options to try and catch the short upswing, but the power move would be buying put options (I will explain those below) because the stock is ultimately falling. As the stock continues going down over the long term, instead of trying to make money catching the small upward bounce back up to resistance, the better strategy would be to profit by buying put options and capitalizing on the stock falling. When a stock is making lower highs and lower lows, it's best not to try to make money on the small upside moves. Using put options is one of our trading secrets on how to profit from stocks that are dropping in value in the short term or long term.

Depending on the market and economy, a stock can create new patterns after a while. A stock that was once uptrending can start to channel sideways, a stock that was channeling sideways can start to downtrend, and any other combinations of the three. That's why it's so important to study the charts, both current and historical. Patterns can change from one to another, signaling when it's time to potentially switch your strategy.

Outside of the three most common, there are 10 other powerful chart patterns that I teach my students. For the other power chart patterns, check out my courses at powertradesuniversity.com.

## THE BEAUTY AND BENEFIT OF OPTIONS— CONTROL VS. OWN

Options are a way to control a stock as opposed to owning a stock. There are two kinds of options: **call options** and **put options**.[3] They can be used to lower your risk and increase your potential profits while also protecting your investment account in the event of a market crash or periods of uncertainty—like the 2008 real estate market crash or when the COVID-19 pandemic hit, causing the world to shut down.

**A call option** lets you control an asset—in this case a stock—for a specific amount of time and allows you to buy it later, if you choose to, at a specific agreed upon price. Call options let you control some of the most expensive stocks for a fraction of the price compared to buying and owning the stock.

The process of buying a call option on a stock can be compared to buying real estate. When you go to buy a house, you put in an offer,

---

3   Lyle Daly, "Call vs. Put Options," Motley Fool, last updated January 5, 2024, https://www.fool.com/investing/how-to-invest/stocks/call-options-vs-put-options/.

and it gets accepted. Say you're looking to buy a $200K house. They ask for earnest money, probably around $2K. With that earnest money, you have 30 days to get an inspection and appraisal before you make your final decision. You've essentially bought a call option on the house because you put $2K down and are controlling a $200K asset (the house) for 30 days.

For illustrative purposes, let's say that after the inspection and appraisal the house comes back valued at $250K.

You've got two choices. Exercise your option, buy the house for $200K, and then turn around and put it back on the market to sell for $250K. Or, take the paper contract you paid $2K for—which is now worth $50K—and sell it to someone else who also wants the house but can't buy it because you have it under contract. Share with them that it's now appraised at $250K. This person, who really wants to move into the house in that neighborhood, is willing to pay $250K for it since it was appraised. So, you can sell them the paper contract for $50K and they use it to buy the house for $200K per the predetermined agreed upon price. To them, they paid a total of $250K.

However, for you, taking that $2K and turning it into $50K by controlling the asset—and never having to come up with that $200K price tag for the house—becomes a $48,000 profit or a 2,400% return using control versus ownership.

You bought an option, and it went up in value because the house was appraised for more within 30 days. The same thing happens with stock—prices can drastically change in your favor in 30 days. Often, the potential for the price to change in your favor can be spotted in the stock chart.

Of course, the opposite can also happen. You get the house appraised and it's only worth $180K. And you say, "I changed my mind. I want to walk away."

It's essentially putting up $2K and having the stock going against you. You lost $2K, but you didn't lose $200K. Rather, you didn't put up $200K and lose $20K because the house was only worth $180K.

That's how call options work. You risk a small amount to control a larger priced asset for a set amount of time with the ability to make a decent amount of money on the upside.

**Put options** are the second type of option. They allow you to strategize to protect your account and even potentially profit from stocks falling. A put option gives you the right to "put" your stock to someone else at a higher price in the event the stock falls during the time the contract is open. Basically, it gives you the right to force someone to buy that stock at a specified price over the next 30, 60, 90 days, etc.

For example, a stock is trading for $200 and you purchased a $190 strike price put option that expires in 30 days. If within 30 days the stock loses value and is selling at $50 because of bad earnings or some negative news, you can force someone to buy the stock at the $190 put option strike price even though it's trading for $50. It would be roughly $140 profit for you minus the price you paid for the put option.

You may be thinking, "Why would someone agree to buy a stock at a later date for a higher price than it's worth if the stock falls?"

Well, it's quite simple. In the market, there are always two sides. In this example, one person doesn't think the stock is going to fall in the next 30 days. They believe they can make some money by selling you a put option because they don't believe they will ever have to fulfill the obligation. You're on the other side of that transaction and believe—based on the stock chart or other information you have—that the stock may be headed lower in the next 30 days. You want to protect your account if you own that stock or try to make money from the stock falling by buying a put option against it.

We do this all the time with car insurance. Let's say you buy a $100K Mercedes or Cadillac. You write a check for $500 a month to your insurance company to have the car insured at $100K. So, you paid $500 for a $100K put option. Your insurance company is the person on the other side of that transaction willing to buy your car for $100K if you crash and total it in the next 30 days. They're willing to take that risk because they read the "stock chart" on you. They like the risk to reward ratio and don't believe—based on the stock chart and data—that you will crash in the next 30 days.

But let's say for whatever reason you did get into an accident, crashed the car, and totaled it. You can force your insurance company to pay $100K for the car, even though the car is now worth $0. What's interesting is that no one asks why the insurance company does that, but when we come over to the stock market it seems like a foreign concept. People wonder why anyone would do that. The reason is, that person is someone who doesn't believe the stock will fall, or in insurance terms, doesn't believe you'll total your car. The real question we should be asking ourselves is, why are we taught to protect depreciating assets like cars but not taught to protect our life savings and investments?

You can protect your portfolio with put options. For example, for $500 a month you can protect your $100K investment account from something like COVID-19, the China trade war, or the 9/11 planes crashing into the World Trade Center where the stock market saw a $1.4 trillion loss in value. If your stock portfolio was at $100K and you had a put option covering the $100K in the event of a crash, you could still force someone to buy your stocks for $100K and make up the money you lost in the crash from your investment account.

So how do insurance companies know who to insure—or, in stock market terms, how do they know which stocks to agree to buy? When you apply for insurance, companies ask basic questions: "Are you married? Do you have kids? Which zip code do you live in? What's your credit score?"

If you're married, you're probably not out drinking and driving. If you have kids, you're probably driving responsibly—certainly not speeding with kids in the backseat. You probably won't be out partying on New Year's Eve, running the risk of getting hit by a drunk driver—in fact, you're more likely to be at home, bringing in the new year safely with the family. If you own a home, you're probably responsible, have a stable income, won't default on the loan, and know how to take care of an expensive asset. Insurance companies also check your credit score. People with a high credit score usually exhibit the traits of a responsible person who makes good decisions that help them avoid accidents.

What you might not realize is that, with stocks, *you* can become the insurance company and the one to collect an extra $500 a month. You might look at a stock like Amazon, for instance, and say, "That stock's not going down. I'll take that calculated risk. I'll take five hundred dollars from you because I don't think Amazon is going to crash into a wall or get hit by a drunk driver and go to zero dollars." In stock market terms, traders who want to profit like an insurance company don't think Jeff Bezos or the leadership team is going to do anything crazy to tank the company. These traders don't see anything in the next 30 days that would stop people from shopping online and enjoying their two-day delivery.

Of course, you were never taught to think like an insurance company—but just remember that traders evaluate stocks in the same way insurance companies evaluate people, risk, and reward, and they can collect monthly premiums on low-risk stocks just as insurance companies collect monthly premiums on low-risk people. Sure, every now and again insurance companies have to pay out a claim, but more often than not, if they're writing policies correctly, they collect more than they have to pay out—and that's the name of the game "collect more than you pay out."

So, in essence, you can use put options in three ways: The first is to insure your investment account in the same way you insure your car; the second is to sell put options and collect monthly premiums, similar to how insurance companies sell insurance; and the third is to buy put options to profit from companies that aren't performing well by capitalizing on their stock prices falling.

For example, if you come across a $50 stock that's not doing well, you can look at the chart to see if it is in a downtrending channel. Then, let's say you pay $4 for a 30-day or longer $45 strike price put. If the stock falls from $50 to $20, you can force someone to buy it at $45, leaving a $25 spread. You effectively turned that $4 put contract into $25 or $21 of pure profit, a 525% return.

When thinking about insuring and protecting your investment account, consider things like how low your investment account can go before it starts affecting your lifestyle and retirement . Buy put options to protect your account so you can sleep well at night knowing that if your account drops below that threshold, you can exercise your put options and make that money back.

If you've got a $100K portfolio that gets below $80K and you believe that's going to mess with your retirement, you can buy an $80K strike price put option or the equivalent put option hedge. If you have a mixed portfolio, you can force someone to buy your stock or portfolio at $80K if it goes below that. You can't lose more than $20K of your $100K portfolio for the time frame you have that put option. You can insure your investment account for 30 days, six months, or a year. When COVID-19 hit, no one knew how long it could last—a year-long put option could ensure you protected your account through something like a pandemic.

When a contract expires, it works like an insurance policy that you can renew for the same price as your previous contract unless something about that stock has changed. In that case, you have to renew based on the new stock or portfolio value. If the stock has moved up and increased in value, a put option for $80K is going to be cheaper. The likelihood of the stock triggering an insurance claim is less likely to happen. For example, if the stock or your portfolio went from $100K to $120K, there is a $40K difference instead of $20K that the stock or your portfolio would have to fall before the $80K put option contract kicks in. But if the stock or your portfolio dropped to $90K, renewing the put option will be more expensive. If you still want to protect your account at $80K, there's more perceived risk because the stock has fallen so close to the put option contract number of $80K.

The option price gets cheaper and cheaper the farther away it gets from the price that would trigger someone being forced to buy or sell the stock. The closer it is to the event happening, the more expensive the option becomes because of the perceived risk. Think of it like a new 16-year-old driver in your household—the insurance company raises your rates because of the perceived risk of a 16-year-old driver who generally is more likely to have more accidents or trigger claim-related events.

You could also think of it in terms of the wildfires in California. If you live 100 miles away from a forest, you can get insurance at a certain rate. If you live 10 miles away from the forest, companies might still insure you, but it will be a lot more expensive. The closer you are to the potential event happening, the more expensive it is. But keep in mind that insurance companies will sometimes deny even writing a policy on high-risk, low-reward situations. You should look at your stocks the same way and stay away from high-risk, high-speculative stocks. Depending on your personal risk level, there will be some stocks you should not be buying or selling calls or puts on because they lack a predictable, repeatable pattern and lack a low-risk, high-reward ratio.

As with any insurance, it's better to buy before an event happens or becomes highly likely to happen. When we heard about COVID-19 spreading from China, we wondered whether it could spread to the U.S. Insurance on stocks and portfolios was cheapest when the virus was across the ocean. As soon as the first confirmed case in the U.S. went public, the stock market started tanking—and when the world began shutting down, insurance (put option prices) went through the roof.

## POWER CHARTS, POWER TRADES, POWER PROFITS

Understanding profitable chart patterns and the use of options led me to **power charts**, **power trades**, and **power profits**—the foundation of my success.

Once you understand how to read stock charts, the next skill to master is the ability to spot **power chart patterns**—like the cup and handle pattern I told you about that allowed me to make $100k in one day. If you don't know how to read stock charts and which patterns you're looking for, you might as well go to the casino because you're guessing and gambling.

By learning how to spot highly predictable, repeatable patterns, you go from guessing to using probability and statistics based on historical data. You're able to forecast where there's support for a stock—where traders believe the stock is oversold and are willing to buy. You can also see resistance—where traders believe a stock is overvalued and are most likely to sell their shares.

When you recognize power chart patterns, you can place a power trade—which takes into account a calculated risk—by asking these questions. One: Am I doing a 1:3 risk reward? Two: Am I putting a lot of power behind this trade by buying a lot of stock or by controlling a lot of stock using options?

Once you recognize the power chart patterns, the next thing to consider is how you place a power trade and take advantage of what you believe is about to happen with the stock. Placing a power trade has several elements to it. It's not about throwing your whole account at some random trade and hoping and praying it works out. Among the things we teach our members in Power Trades University is to calculate the risk reward. Ideally you want to take trades that have a 1:3 risk reward ratio. In other words, if I'm going to risk $1, the chart better tell me this trade has the potential to make $3.

Now, when it comes to putting power behind the trade, there are two ways to do it. In the ENPH example I mentioned earlier, you could buy 1.3 million dollars of shares of a company. But if you don't have $1.3 million to buy the shares, the second way you can put a lot of power behind your trade is to buy the equivalent of $1.3 million shares in options and control the stock for a defined period of time.

In the ENPH example, even if you had $1.3 million, putting $200K up to control the same $1.3 million would leave you with $1.1 million left to trade in the event that something went horribly wrong. On the flip side, if you don't have $1.3 million, you still have the ability to play the same game as someone who does have that kind of buying power but for a fraction of the cost. Equally important to remember is that there are ways to protect your account from going to zero regardless of whether you choose to buy the shares of stock or control the shares with options in the event that you are wrong and the stock goes against you. We'll get more into those protection strategies in later chapters.

**Power profit** is all about your money having the power to work harder and smarter for you compared to how hard you can work for your money. (Remember my earlier example of my making $100K in a single day versus working a year of 40- to 60-hour work weeks to earn it.) It's having your money produce returns above and beyond what you could trade hours in a day for. When power profit trades happen, don't be greedy—be grateful and sell your stock options to lock in your profit.

Most people don't get a 50% return on their investments. You don't get trades like that every day but it's so powerful that when you get them once or twice, it's life changing.

**Power charts**: understanding powerful chart patterns and how to profit from them is all about identifying predictable, repeatable buy-and-sell patterns.

**Power trade**: putting a lot of power behind a trade by buying the stock. Or, for those who don't have millions of dollars, learning which option strategy to use—calls or puts—to control the stock so you can get a powerful return.

**Power profit**: having your money work hard for you—making the same amount or more in a shorter period of time than it would normally take you to earn in a year or a 30-day time frame.

Although the power trade system can create unique and awesome results, it has to be coupled with self-mastery. You cannot be a power trader without the power of discipline. Discipline is mastering fear and greed and making sure you don't blow up your account so you can live to trade another day.

**CHAPTER 3: TAKEAWAYS**

- Options have the ability to give you exponentially higher returns.
- The three most common chart patterns are uptrending channeling, downtrending channeling, and sideways channeling.
- You can control higher priced stocks for a fraction of the cost with call options.
- You can protect your account from major losses with put options.
- You can make money like the insurance companies with put options.

CHAPTER 4

# You Never Go Broke Taking a Profit

**As I reflect on my** trading journey back to when my cousin and I stopped putting in the work to be successful and stopped doing the research, I would experience another school of hard knocks mistake that I hope to prevent you from ever having to go through. There was a gorgeous downtown condo in Royal Oak, Michigan, at "The Fifth," the building I wanted to live in. I was enamored by this building back in the day and took a tour of one of the units with its brick columns running through it, floor-to-ceiling windows, a divider wall with a fireplace on either side, and a view all the way to downtown Detroit. There was a doorman out front, a gym on site, and some pro athletes even lived there. For me, it represented one of the ultimate living spots in one of the coolest cities—a building with interesting people doing interesting things. This building to me represented that you were making a certain amount of money and able to maintain a certain lifestyle. That was the motivation behind wanting to live there.

That condo felt like the ultimate bachelor pad, the ultimate "F-U" to my old life—going from a home with bars on the windows to one with floor-to-ceilings windows, from looking over my shoulder hoping I don't get robbed to sitting in a high-rise with a bird's eye view over the city. I saw that condo as a triumph over a life of poverty. I thought, "Why not go for it? Let's keep this party and lifestyle going," or maybe, "Let's take this party and lifestyle to another level," by upgrading my living situation.

I'd always understood that if you own something outright, if you can cash something out, it's less likely that it can be taken from you. You lock in a higher standard of living and things like taxes and utilities are chump change. My thought was, "Let's do it and lock it in by paying cash."

My account was at $250,000 and I needed an additional $500,000 for the condo. I wanted to be able to pay cash for it and still have a quarter million left to trade. I saw an opportunity to generate that type of cash on a trade with Yahoo's stock ticker symbol YHOO and decided to invest the entire account all in on one trade.

One of the problems that some traders get into is that they don't see the actual trade or risk. They see themselves spending that money, living in that house, driving that car. They aren't paying attention to the chart or how high the stock can go. Even worse, they're not paying attention to what could happen if the trade goes against them. That was me. While I was mentally counting and spending money I hadn't made yet on the Yahoo trade, I wasn't reading the chart. I saw half a million dollars profit—I wasn't paying attention to the patterns. The only thing on my mind was getting the money and buying that condo, and that's how greed starts.

I now know it's important to pay attention to the chart. **Get out when the chart tells you to get out**. Yes, you may have a rough idea of how much money you plan to make, but you have to be prepared to pivot if things go against you. Instead of thinking strategically with my risk management hat on, I was thinking, "Five hundred thousand, this is how much I'm going to make," without confirming in the charts whether the stock had the probability of going to that level or had the capability of producing that kind of financial return.

That mindset was one piece—along with no longer doing my research with my cousin—of what led to my downfall early on. My eyes and mind filled with greed of making half a million dollars and buying the condo. I never thought for a second that I could lose the money.

At some point in that trade, I was up $100K and could have gotten out, but that wasn't enough to pay cash for the condo, so I didn't do it. I wanted it to go up more. Then it started to tank. When a trade goes against you, you go through different emotional stages. It starts with hope and then moves to prayer.

**There is no room for hope and prayer in the stock market. God is neutral on the trade. He's not sending it up or down.**

When the trade went down, my account dropped by about $75K and I started hoping it would go back up. Then it went down again, and I was down about $150K. I kept telling myself I'd give it a little more time to turn around. Then it went down by $200K. I started praying that it would go back up—forget profit, I just wanted to break even at this point. "Please let it go back up so I can get my money back."

It never really occurred to me that I should cut my losses and get out. It got to a point where I started bargaining with God and the market. "Please, let me make my money back. I'll do right on the next trade, and I promise I'll go to church next Sunday."

Then it got to the point where I thought it would be worthless. I cut my loss at about $150K and only had about $100K left.

## TRADE THE CHART, NOT YOUR BANK ACCOUNT

After I lost a good portion of my account, I came up with one of many sayings that would have helped me in this situation: **trade the chart, not your bank account.**

Forget about watching your trading account go up and down. That's a horrible way to make decisions. If you're down $1K or $10K, don't think about the account, look at the chart. Is the chart telling you to sell? I've seen people sell when the chart says the stock is getting ready to bounce and go higher. I've also seen people hold on to stocks longer than they should when the chart says "sell"—all because they were watching their bank account and not the chart.

Still thinking in terms of making my money back, I went into another trade in WorldCom where I put in $75K. I was up $100K in that one. A friend of mine who was also trading in WorldCom asked if we should get out. I said, "Nah, this stock is going to give me all my money back." Then, within only two hours, we watched the stock take my account up to $100K, then drop all the way back down. We texted back and forth to try to figure out what to do. We were paralyzed. We saw the money, thought it was ours when the stock was up, but it wasn't because we didn't get out. By the way, the money is never really yours until you sell.

In my head, I didn't want to get out until it went back up to $100K—I wasn't getting out until I saw that money back. But I still didn't confirm in the chart whether the stock had that potential to go back up.

By this time, I wasn't in control of my emotions, cycling through fear and greed. I lost another $50K on that trade, more or less, and was down to about $25K. That's when I decided to take the $25K and pay off my bills until I could figure out my next move. It was all I had left before I ran out of money.

I did some small trades to get $1K here and $5K there, but there was no way to claw myself out of the hole I had dug with these smaller profits. Eventually I took another $10K hit to my trading account. My mental state was disbelief and panic: "Does this still work? Am I even good enough to do this?"

A whole range of unhealthy thoughts had started to enter my brain. It takes a certain amount of confidence and belief to be successful in the stock market game—it doesn't work if you start questioning whether you have what it takes or start thinking the stock market is rigged. When you're making trades off hope, emotions, and gambling—and not by paying attention to the charts—then you've left the skills of managing risk and reward behind and are now in the Wild West. You start to believe you're cursed or that the market has something against you personally. Is it because of that one time I stole something from a store and didn't get caught? Is it karma? Trading when you're not in the right mental space is the worst thing you can do.

My stomach was starting to hurt too. Every time I pressed the button to buy, I was thinking, "I know it's going to go against me." My brain held nothing but negative thoughts toward the trade and the market. I started playing mind games with myself, thinking that if I sold something it would go up just to spite me and if I bought the stock, it would drop—so I ended up doing the opposite of what I really wanted to do.

It's ridiculous, but it's these fearful thought patterns that make you play silly games and ultimately turn a situation like mine from bad to worse. It's one of the worst places to be, mentally.

**Technically, in a bad situation like this you should step away from the market and stop trading. Practice trading with virtual or fake money. After you build a winning track record, you can re-enter the market with real money on small trades and work your way back to your previous level of trading as you rebuild your confidence.**

Looking back, if I had taken a profit the first time, I'd be at $350K. If I did it the second time, I'd have had $450K and be in a much better place. Instead, I didn't take the profit and I was tainted by the twin emotional monsters in the market that eventually wipe everyone out—fear and greed.

Greed took me out the first time when I was focused on buying that condo. Then fear the second time, when I was afraid to push the button to buy stocks or options. I pushed it when I shouldn't and was afraid to push it when I should.

It wasn't until I stepped away from investing and took a real pause to reflect that I figured out what went wrong. I asked myself, "What would Warren Buffett do?" If he had quit after a major loss, he never would have become Warren Buffett. He probably looked back to see what he did wrong and never did it again. I'm sure he got his two rules for investing after a big loss that made him pause and reflect before getting into the game again. Rule 1: Don't lose money. Rule 2: Don't forget Rule 1.

## LIVE TO TRADE ANOTHER DAY

As I rebuilt my account, I started reflecting. I looked at how I was up in that trade and didn't take the money. That's when one of my rules and core principles became clear to me: **you never go broke taking a profit**. Had I taken the profit when I was up in the Yahoo trade or the WorldCom trade, I wouldn't have gone broke.

I started looking at the emotions I experienced too—fear and greed—and dissected them as I began to trade again. When I saw I was up, I chose to close out profitable trades, not wanting to relive those moments again of watching all my profits evaporate. I also wanted to show myself that I had mastered control over greed. I started with smaller trades as I got into the game again, and by the time I worked my way up to larger trades, those principles were ingrained in me.

When I'm up in a profitable trade, I often say to myself, "I'm a good trader and what do good traders do? Take the profit." If the stock went higher after I sold it, I would remind myself that "you never go broke taking a profit." I would be okay if I didn't get the last drop of profit as long as I didn't go broke again.

Any time I go into a trade, I know where I want to sell and where I'll get out if it goes against me. I have a target profit and, ideally, I plan to get out around 10 to 25% below that point—I don't expect the stocks to rise perfectly. So, for example, if I think I can make $100K, I'm happy with $75K or at least I'm planning to exit when I'm up $75k.

Equally as important, I factor an "I'm Wrong" level into every trade. I have a plan to get out of a trade if it goes against me and drops below a certain threshold. I didn't have an "I'm Wrong" level with Yahoo. I told myself it would go up and I'd break even. Same with WorldCom. Neither went back up. It never occurred to me back then that I could be wrong. Now I ask myself with every trade, "What if I'm wrong?" So, when putting money into a trade, I know where I'll get out. That way I'm not telling myself, "Oh, I'll give it a little more time to turn around." I'll take a small loss rather than risk a catastrophic loss. This allows me to overcome those two emotions—fear and greed.

Another one of my phrases is: **live to trade another day**. Had I got out when I was down $50K and still had $200K, I could have lived to trade another day. But I didn't. Now, I go into every trade thinking, "What if I'm wrong? What if it hits that level?" If it hits that level, I'm shutting it down. I don't reset my "I'm Wrong" level, I cut my losses. Shutting a trade down is important for resetting your emotions.

When Yahoo fell, I kept resetting my "I'm Wrong" level, telling myself, "It'll go back up, we'll be okay, we'll give it more time." I kept moving it lower until there was almost nothing to move. Now, I get out and let my emotions reset. I look at the chart and ask myself, "Would you buy right here, right now based on this chart?"

**Looking at the chart and stock as a brand-new trade allows you to break the emotional chain. When you're in it, you're trading your bank account again.** You're telling yourself, "I want to break even." The chart doesn't have your emotions or desires on it. The chart has prices and data—your job is to interpret that data to see if it can reach a point where you also break even. In the big picture, your job is to read the chart and if it says it's not going back to break-even or hits your "I'm Wrong" level, you have to act according to the chart—not your bank account—and get out before you have no account left.

So, now I don't negotiate with the stock market if it hits my "I'm Wrong" level. If it hits it, I'm out. That helps me break the emotional chain and allows me to live to trade another day and look at the trade with fresh eyes if I choose to go back in.

With my big $100K profit trade with ENPH, the stock increased by $3, but I only needed it to go up $2. As soon as it hit the $2 increase, I sold and exited the trade. I wasn't waiting around until the end of the day to see if the stock would go higher. I don't play that game anymore. It all goes back to mastering greed and the principle that you never go broke taking a profit. I could have been bummed that I missed that extra $50K to $100K with the $3 increase, but I reminded myself that I was happy with what I had.

Think about it like this—would you rather go into your next trade with a win or a loss? Would you rather go into your next trade with the same or less money? Or would you rather go into the next trade with the profit from your previous trade paying for it? For me I'd rather go into the next trade with a win that helps my confidence and the funding from the profit off my previous trade.

You don't want to play the game of "How high can it go?" That's a horrible game to play because you never know where or when it will end. "How high can it go?" is not a strategy. It's a gamble. You can never become a consistently profitable trader or make a living off the stock market by trying to perfectly pick the top of every trade. It's like saying you have a special ability to pick that last day, hour, and minute that the stock is done going up and you can milk the trade for every penny you can get out of it. You think you can do that consistently? That's an incredibly cocky mindset and way of living.

That was me—a cocky mindset is what knocked me out. "I'm going to make half a million." I thought it was written in stone and I was basically ready to go to the condo and sign the paperwork to buy it in cash.

Now I say, "I'm projected to make half a million. But if I'm wrong, I'm getting out."

You have to know the difference between gambling and strategic trading and investing. You can use the stock market to gamble, or you can use it to take high-probability, calculated, low-risk, high-reward trades. What I have a problem with is people coming into this industry dropping $1K on a random trade without looking at a chart, doing any research, or having any risk and reward calculations and calling it investing and trading. They might as well be buying $1K in lottery tickets.

If someone tells you that you should invest in a particular stock, your answer should be, "No, no, no, no!" if you don't understand it. That's not an investment, that's a gamble. You wouldn't know what to do when and if it goes against you. **If you don't know why you're investing in a stock, know the risks, or know when to get out, you shouldn't be investing or trading.**

A good trade for one person isn't a good trade for someone else. Any investment you don't understand is a bad investment. If you're the one saying, "I heard this is the thing to buy," then you're gambling.

These are the lessons I learned after going broke, which is why I preach that you never go broke taking a profit. Since I went broke, I had to get a job and in getting a job, I had to deal with some new realities.

## YOUR BOSS IS NOT YOUR ENEMY

When I had to go back into the workforce, I was initially angry that entrepreneurship and investing didn't work out. I was disappointed that I was back to working weekends and mad that I had a cap on my earnings. But even with all the disappointment and negative feelings, I had a strategic game plan I had to execute. I was no longer riding on my "I can print as much money as I want from the stock market" high horse and I had to learn not only to survive but to thrive in corporate America, a world I once hated.

I understood sales and I'd worked in the mobile phone industry before, so I set my eyes on getting a job in that field. My game plan was to get a job with a decent hourly wage or salary that I could live on while making a commission to pay down debt and get back into investing. When I interviewed for a job at Verizon, my soon-to-be manager asked if I could perform a certain set of tasks and skills.

She said, "We need you to provide this level of customer service, hit your sales goals by selling this many mobile phone units, work weekends and some holidays." I said, "Yes, I can and will do that for the dollar amount you're offering, and I will be better than any other candidates you're interviewing." You see, when I was flat broke, although I was frustrated and disappointed, there was also a part of me that was happy to get a job, have a steady paycheck, and get back on my feet—not to mention the mobile phone discount and tuition reimbursement that allowed me to go back to school. Although this was not where I ultimately wanted to be, I had to make the best of the situation. To put it another way, I had to take this opportunity to chart my way back to the stock market and financial freedom.

My work ethic, energy, and attitude changed. It wasn't my manager's or the company's responsibility to make me rich or lead me to financial freedom. It was their job to pay me a fair wage for fair work, a wage that we both agreed upon. Nowhere in the contract did it say my manager or Verizon would help me achieve financial freedom. They didn't say, "We will help you with work-life balance, we will help you drive the car of your dreams." None of that was in the contract. That part was my responsibility. So, while I started to work hard for Verizon, I simultaneously went to work hard on my personal plan for achieving my dreams and goals.

Part of my personal plan was to become more valuable in the corporate marketplace—both to employers and myself. I would set goals to be the top sales rep and work my way to becoming a supervisor and eventually a manager. I figured that learning new skills for managing people alongside my sales skills would serve me well and make me more valuable in the marketplace.

As I worked my way up the corporate ladder, I was also taking advantage of tuition reimbursement and taking classes at Wayne State University's Mike Ilitch School of Business. Since I had some experience with the stock market, I figured I'd go back to school to get a degree in finance. This was all part of my plan to make myself more valuable both personally and professionally.

After getting into management, earning my degree, and eventually returning to the stock market, I decided it was time to leave Verizon and go into trading full-time. Although I was excited to walk away, I still had war wounds from the last time I quit my job. Shortly after leaving Verizon, I started to lose money in the stock market. I thought to myself, "Oh no! I'm not going through this again." So, I decided to get a job roughly six months later, this time as an account manager with Comcast. I wanted to take time figuring out why I was losing money in the market. Having an income that allowed me to pay my bills meant I wouldn't feel forced to trade.

I worked my way up the corporate ladder at Comcast to becoming a regional manager, overseeing Target, Best Buy, Verizon, and other accounts like Walmart stores. I had my account executives working under me, managing anywhere from 30 to 50 stores each. In total, at any given time, we had somewhere between 300 to 500 stores we were overseeing. I finally felt like I had made it in the corporate world. I had a big title, a six-figure salary, and I somewhat controlled my own schedule. Life was good until I was hit with a dose of reality.

It was Thanksgiving eve. I was sitting at the table with family and received a phone call from my manager. He wanted to discuss Black Friday and make sure the team and I were prepared and had everything we needed.

I told him that all the stores were good to go. I'd had a meeting with my team. Everyone knew where they needed to be and were trained up. Everyone was in place.

He paused and said, "Okay, what store are you going to?"

"Oh, I didn't realize you wanted me out in the field." I had hit a couple of stores already to make sure merchandising and promos were in place and everything was set for Black Friday.

Again, he said, "Oh, okay, but what stores are you going to visit?"

"I guess I'll start out at the Utica store and make my way around Metro Detroit and make sure our high traffic stores get a visit."

I was super irritated I was a regional manager, a super high position, and I was still visiting stores on Black Friday. Still out in the field. This one phone call brought back so much trauma from all the holidays and weekends I'd spent in the stores working in retail for Mervyn's, Best Buy, Sprint PCS, and Verizon, missing family events and never enjoying the holidays.

As irritated as I was at my boss, it wasn't his fault. It was his job to make sure I delivered the numbers. He was not my enemy. He was not holding me back. I had gone through the system, starting from sales rep at Verizon and working my way into leadership, then moving over to Comcast, becoming an account manager, then finally a regional manager. It wasn't my boss that was the problem. It was the system.

I'd agreed to work in that system and that's how the system is set up. You always have someone to answer to. You'll never own the company. You'll always have to work weekends and holidays in retail sales. Sales are down and they need to cut heads, you could be one of the first on the chopping block. That's how the corporate retail system works.

With that realization, I stopped being mad at my boss. If I didn't like the system, I had to create my own.

They gave me a job and a salary plus benefits. They didn't say in the interview, "Well, if you don't want to work Black Friday, you don't have to." Or "If your kids are sick, take as much time as you need, go be at home with them." Or "If you want to go to your kid's graduation, you don't have to worry about the sales numbers." Or "Oh, if you and your wife are getting divorced because you're never at home, we'll give you an extra two weeks of vacation." Those things were not in the contract.

We often forget what we initially agreed to and, when life happens, we think the corporate system owes us something. The corporate system was designed for one thing—to make the owners and shareholders a profit. That's not a bad thing, I run a company now too. The point is that anything outside of your work agreement—things like work-life balance, spending time with your family, driving your dream car—are your responsibility to figure out and not your boss's or employer's responsibility.

It was clear that the corporate world was using me to produce a specific result, and I wanted to use them to make money to pay down my debts and get back into investing. In the meantime, I was learning how to build my own system by getting on-the-job leadership and business training. We were not enemies. They needed me and I needed them. I was going to take the money I made from them and invest it. And I was going to use my on-the-job business training to get out of their system and into my own.

I learned how a Fortune 50 company operates, hit their numbers, deliver earnings, and deliver results. I learned from working on the inside, by watching how those companies operate with respect to sales and customer service. I learned to differentiate between a good company and a bad one. This skillset made me an even better stocks and option trader when it came to analyzing companies I didn't work for and determining if I wanted to invest in them.

## MAKING THE SYSTEM WORK FOR YOU

When it comes to feeling like you're not getting paid enough by a company, you can change your mindset to, "I already agreed to this, and now that I'm in the system, how do I use it to put myself and my family in a better situation? How do I use this as leverage to become a better employee and become more valuable to myself and the marketplace?"

The way I looked at the employee/employer relationship is that the best employees get raises and make more money. Then you get to take that money and put it into a system that doesn't restrict you with not being able to work 24 hours a day, not being able to make more than the salary agreed to, and having to wait for your boss to recognize your hard work before you get a raise. I worked hard in a system that I basically had a love/hate relationship with to get back into a system that I had a love/love relationship with—investing I became the best employee. My boss wasn't my enemy. The company wasn't my enemy.

**Being the best that you can be allows you other opportunities.**

People think that because they hate their job, they can clock in late, do the bare minimum of work, and just skate by. Maybe they'll pretend to be ill and call in sick from work on a Saturday if they partied too hard on Friday night, but they don't understand that 1) they'll be making less money toward getting out of that corporate system if they're out of sick leave and 2) they can't bring those bad habits into the stock market and expect to win. **The stock market takes positive habits like research, getting up early, self-discipline, and handling and controlling emotions to be successful.**

I've seen people getting mad at their boss and deciding, "Oh, I'm going to go in there and quit. I'm going to quit on Friday so they will be short-handed and screwed over the weekend." Usually, you just end up screwing yourself over by acting that way. Try calling that manager or company back for a reference for future employment. Good luck getting a positive referral.

That's not something that someone with a good work ethic or integrity does. If you bring that same attitude to the stock market, you'll get eaten alive. It takes consistency, persistence, and diligence. If things aren't going your way, you can't fire the stock market or quit and hope it screws them—you'll screw yourself.

If you build those bad habits and exhibit reckless behavior at a corporate job, you'll have almost no chance of coming to the stock market and being successful. You'll stroll in with those bad habits and reckless behavior and it'll cost you your entire account.

I tell listeners of my Five-Year Millionaire podcast that your habits follow you everywhere you go. If you're someone who steps on the gas every time a traffic light turns yellow to see if you can beat it before it turns red, that's a low-reward, high-risk trade. If you beat the yellow light, you get to your destination two seconds early. If you're wrong and the light turns red before you get through, another car could enter the intersection and you could crash. It could kill you, passengers in your car, the driver of the other car. That is a horrible risk versus reward trade to take. Reward: save two seconds of time. Risk: total your car, potential paralysis, kill other people or yourself. If you're a person who does that, you might be the person thinking, "How high can this stock go?" "Let's get this meme stock." "Bitcoin sounds good because I heard it's the future."

You bring that same mentality with you to the stock market—trying to run yellow lights with no real reward and high risk—and you wonder why the stock market doesn't work for you. You can't figure out why you're losing money. There are many decisions in real life that parallel those you make in investing or trading in the stock market. You can easily see why some people are frustrated with the market or make horrible investing decisions—no patience, no ability to calculate risk versus reward, and gambling with their life and their life savings.

Do you think you can come over to the stock market and be successful when you haven't learned to navigate some of life's basic decisions—especially those that involve risk versus reward? People who think that way are their own worst enemy in the stock market. You must have a good work ethic at your job or you're not going to have a good work ethic in the stock market. Many things in life—fear, greed, gambling, running red lights, sleeping in on Saturdays—can translate into someone not being willing to wake up early and look at the charts to prepare for the stock market opening on Monday.

It's not only about making money—it's about being a better person. It's highly improbable you'll succeed in investing as a horrible person with a horrible work ethic. A simple shift in mindset can literally change your life and financial success.

## DOING WHAT NEEDS TO BE DONE

While I was working to rebuild my account and had a job that helped me put more money into the stock market machine, I chose to live below my means. If it didn't involve food or shelter, I cut it out of my life. When you've lived a high-level life in the past and are trying to get back there as fast as possible, all that matters is getting back. Everything else that doesn't support that mission is a distraction. When you've made $100K, making anything less is unacceptable because you know what's possible. If you did it once, you can do it again.

My mindset was that I needed every dollar to go into getting me a $250K account or better. Nothing else was important—clothes, hanging out, or partying. I thought, "Do I want to party now and pay for it later or do I want to sacrifice now so that I can party and live most people can't later?"

It wasn't hard to make the sacrifice. I saw people who were 40 and 50 who were still working in retail, working every weekend as a manager or sales rep. There's nothing wrong with making a good, honest living at a full-time job like that, but I knew that wasn't my ideal future and that if I didn't change something, I would be in the same situation, working weekends and holidays in retail standing on my feet all day.

While I lived at my mother's house during my first rebuilding stage, I would think about conversations I had with people in the workplace where I held different jobs. I noticed Person A would make $45K, for example, and say, "I don't know how anyone lives off a penny less." I would talk to Person B, another employee with the same lifestyle and family circumstances who makes $55K and this person would say, "I'm broke after every paycheck. I don't know how anyone lives off anything less than this."

I would think to myself, "What happened to the ten-thousand dollar difference in their salaries? They live in the same town, so their cost of living should be similar—both have no kids or a spouse."

It became clear to me that the difference is there's at least $10K of sacrifice that Person B could make and probably some additional sacrifices that Person A could make, but neither of them are willing or know how to make that sacrifice and put the money into something that could create a brighter financial future like the stock market.

I wasn't going to be like Person A or Person B. I chose to live below my means and invest the surplus to reach my goals.

I often talk to people who tell me they wish they could do what I do. I say, "You can. Sell everything you own and move back in with your mom."

"Oh, no, I can't do that."

"Why not?"

If you really think about it and chisel away at it, why can't you? The top two things I usually hear back are 1) "We would kill each other." Okay, so a sacrifice you're not willing to make is figuring out how to get along with your mother. And 2) "What will people think? What will I tell my friends?" No, no, I asked if you could sell your stuff and move back in with your mom. The answer to that is yes. So, you could literally and physically make the sacrifice to get the money to put in the stock market. No one ever said, "The stock market only works if you know what you're going to tell your friends about why you sold all your stuff and moved back in with your mother."

It works when you know what sacrifices you're willing to make to get the money and—after you make those sacrifices—to get the knowledge to know what to do with the money.

For me, the pain of not having my old good lifestyle was way heavier than worrying about what I was going to tell my friends. Some people have to go through that "rock bottom" experience to find out what they're willing to sacrifice when they're forced to let go of things. Wouldn't it be something if people "decided" they were going to go through that on their own. They didn't need to hit rock bottom. They chose to live below their means on purpose and with a plan.

"Oh, I can afford the car, but I downsized on purpose. I could afford the house, but I chose to get a roommate or move back to my mother's house as part of a bigger plan that's going to set me up for the rest of my life" versus, "Oh, I'm down on my luck, what am I going to tell everyone to cover it up?" Which statement and mindset has more power and more control?

Once I got the job with Verizon, I could have moved out of my mom's house and into my own place. I could have kept up the status quo look on the outside, but I would have been living paycheck to paycheck and would never have gotten back into the stock market as quickly. I purposefully accepted staying at my mother's house as long as I did as part of the game plan to cut all expenses beyond food and shelter, and I even wanted to keep my shelter bill as low as possible.

So ask yourself, are you willing to be the best employee and develop the skills that will assist you in the market? Are you willing to live below your means as you make more money and have your money work harder for you instead of you working harder for it? Are you willing to make lifestyle sacrifices and create a financial margin to invest? Are you willing to get back on the stock market horse even if you blew up your account before?

Because that's what I did.

**CHAPTER 4: TAKEAWAYS**

- You never go broke taking a profit. When you're up, sell and take the money.
- Trade the chart, not your bank account. Make your decisions based on what the chart is telling you.
- Prayer and hope are not strategies.
- Live to trade another day. Do not blow up your account.
- The company you work for and your boss are not your enemies.
- The stock market imitates life.

CHAPTER 5

# Is the Stock Market a Scam?

**Remember in Chapter 1 when** I told you about my first experience buying Sprint stock at $5, then watching it drop to $4, and then channeling back and forth between $4 and $5?

I felt like the market had a personal vendetta against me. I thought it was a scam. After I pressed the button to buy, "they" got all my info, social security number, and cell phone, saw who owns the stock at what price, and wouldn't let it go any higher. They're not going to let the little guy make any money.

When the stock dropped back down to $4, I was pissed. I couldn't believe it. I was certain the market was rigged, that there was a man behind the curtain not letting it go past $5. I later found that the market wasn't rigged. It wasn't a scam. There was no man behind the curtain watching me—but in the moment, it sure felt that way.

When we don't understand something, the safe or default response is, "It's a scam. It's rigged." It's a self-protection method. No one wants to say, "I don't understand how it works," or "Maybe I did something wrong," so they default to blaming something or someone else. "I'm not wealthy because of the Republicans." "I'd have more money if the Democrats weren't in office." "I don't have a job because of the government." No one says, "Maybe it's because I haven't taken the time to learn how to invest. Maybe it's because I'm not financially responsible. Maybe it's because my skillset is outdated."

With the Sprint stock, it took me about a month to recognize and understand the pattern I was seeing and finally make my first $100 in the stock market. The stock didn't fall a dollar a day, it fell in 10- to 20-cent increments and moved up in those same small increments. I didn't realize it at the time, but if I had drawn out the price action of the stock on a piece of paper, it would have looked like a snake or a ball bouncing between $4 and $5. I later found that this pattern was called a "channeling stock." I got really good at getting in at $4 and out at $5 several times a month not fully realizing I was playing this pattern. I was bringing in about $100 every other week, $200 a month.

After a few months of playing that channeling pattern on Sprint stock, I started wondering what other patterns existed out there and what other stocks were moving in a similar pattern. As I found other stocks that moved similarly, I also found new stock patterns to trade—but I realized these stocks were *way* outside of my price range. I would need more money to take advantage of other stock patterns to make more money between the up and down cycles.

If I was doing this well trading with $500, what could I do if I had $5K or $10K, I wondered? But how was I supposed to get that type of investment and trading capital? The stocks I was looking at were out of my price range at about $100 a share. With my original $500, I would only be able to buy five shares, and a stock would need to move substantially to make any real money.

## FROM "RIGGED" TO "STRATEGY"

I started thinking about how I could get more money into the machine. I thought if I did the same thing I did with Sprint, if I had $1K, I could make $200 every other week. If I had $10K, I'd be rich.

At this point, some of the things I'd learned about personal development and finance started to make sense because of the multi-level marketing (MLM) I was involved with—like using other people's money. But whose money could I borrow?

As I shared earlier, many of my friends had student loan refund checks that they used for partying, apartment rent, and other things, and I thought maybe I could make student loan money work for me. My scholarship at Wayne State University's Mike Ilitch School of Business covered tuition and books but not room and board. I lived at home, but no one needed to know that. Besides, we were technically poor enough to qualify for the student loan even with the scholarship—and that's when I got what I thought was a genius idea. I went the route of applying for student loans, knowing I would get a refund check because my tuition was covered by a scholarship. In my head, I was like, "Bingo, that's how I'm going to get the ten thousand dollars to put into the stock market." That was my "Aha!" moment. Now I could play the same game with a larger amount of money.

As I learned more and more about the stock market and patterns, I saw that the stock market isn't rigged. It doesn't have a personal vendetta against me. I began to see that there were price levels at which people liked the stock and didn't like the stock, and that if you draw out that data on a piece of paper, you can see the patterns and price points.

Eventually, I realized you can search for those patterns in the stock market by learning how to read stock charts. Once I understood it wasn't rigged or didn't have anything against me personally, I got excited about the stock market because I knew that if I could see which stocks—at what price—the big money investors and big institution traders liked and didn't like, then I could participate in buying low and selling high at the most ideal times.

**Follow the big money**. The "big money" folks can't resist buying a stock if it's at a good price. They don't have the ability to hide that. You can almost see where big money from institutions or traders is pouring in. You can also see where they're thinking, "This stock is getting overvalued," or "This is getting too risky, we already got the return we wanted, maybe we should unload and look for the next stock."

When I could see that in the chart patterns, I was hooked! I was working at Sprint and selling phones, but I was browsing the web on my own cell phone, looking at prices go up and down, excited to get home and plot it on paper.

Manually, old-school, on paper, I'd take the data, draw it out, and connect the dots. I could see where the stock was going between two price points by going through the patterns. That process marked my transition from thinking I was being scammed and that the market was rigged to knowing it was about patterns.

When I found a new one, I'd trade it. It got to a point where a $10K investment account wasn't enough. I would find multiple trades I wanted to be in at the same time, and I wondered, "How do I do this on a bigger scale? How can I do two or three trades?" One trade would take all my money and then I was stuck waiting and watching other opportunities pass me by.

Some of the best stocks I looked at were $100 to $400 a share back then, and at the time, that seemed ridiculously expensive for my small trading account. I would ask myself how I could trade into the bigger, more expensive, high-growth, high-potential for return stocks. That's when my cousin and I started to explore options and the concept of controlling stock versus owning the stock. That allowed us to play the patterns on bigger stocks without having a big account.

I went from being pissed off and irritated to motivated and excited. All I wanted to do was look at stock charts. People would ask, "That's got to be boring, isn't it? I would be bored to death." It wasn't boring to me. I didn't see lines and numbers going up and down on a boring piece of paper. I saw money. In life, we're taught that a picture is worth a thousand words. In the stock market, I learned that a picture—stock chart—is worth thousands of dollars. After I got really good at identifying the channeling stock pattern, I started wondering what other patterns were out there.

I learned that the Sprint pattern I recognized was one of many. On CNBC and other investment shows, they talked about different patterns I had never heard of like cup and handles or head and shoulders.

I had no idea what the names meant, but I understood that there were all kinds of patterns that I could be making money from.

## TECHNICAL TRADING

I became a technical trader. I didn't care about the fundamentals or earnings. All I cared about was the technical data on the chart. It was like checking the weather—technically, do I care whether it's cumulus clouds that are overhead or exactly where the cold front and warm front are coming together? No. Technically, I just want to look at that graph and see what the chances of rain or sunshine are for today or for the week. So, I'm a technical trader, not a fundamental trader.

The fundamentals upon doing my initial stock analysis didn't really matter to me because whatever they were, they would show up in the chart. Like rain. It doesn't matter what kind of cloud it is—it'll show up on the chart as rain. As long as I could read the weather map, I could tell that rain was coming. If a stock was in a downtrend, I could see by looking at the stock chart that the fundamentals must not be good. I didn't have to research the fundamentals first. If they were good, the stock for the most part would be in an uptrend. **The chart is the key to everything. It's like the CliffsNotes version of how a company is doing.**

People ask, "How's that company doing?"

"Well, let's look at the chart."

"Don't you want to know what they sell?"

"No. The chart will give me the big picture of how well they're doing."

After that, I can look into the fundamentals of why they're doing well or badly. For the most part, the chart tells me the majority of what I need to know or at least gives me a starting point, telling me what I need to research after I've determined whether the stock is in an up, down, or sideways trend.

People read charts every day. On our phones, we read weather charts. In hospitals, we look at the chart and pattern on heart rate monitors. You don't need to go to school and get a degree to understand the weather app on your phone. You don't question, "How do they know it's going to rain today? What if this is a mistake?" You trust the data in the chart. You don't need to know how they send the data from a tower to your phone and add in the color graphics.

Stock charts are very similar—you don't need to understand every little detail. When you look at the chart, you can tell if the stock is going up or going down. Later, you can dig into why. You can get more details. But for the big picture, you can look at a chart and tell which direction the stock is going.

Earlier, I showed you line charts that give you a high-level view of the direction a stock is moving and tells you whether the stock closed up or down from the previous day. There are different types of charts that tell you different things. There's a **line chart**, a **bar chart**, and my personal favorite is the **candlestick chart**. Different charts show different ways to interpret the same kinds of data with less or more information than others.

A **line chart** connects closing points to each other at the end of a day. It takes the closing price, plots it out, and then draws a line to connect it to the closing price of the previous day. The line chart gives you a limited amount of information. You can see when a stock goes up and down each day and throughout the week. But it doesn't tell you if the stock opened higher in the morning and sold off during the day. It also doesn't tell you if it opened lower, ran up due to people buying, and then sold off back down. A line chart does not give you any intra-day data, it only tells you where it closed.

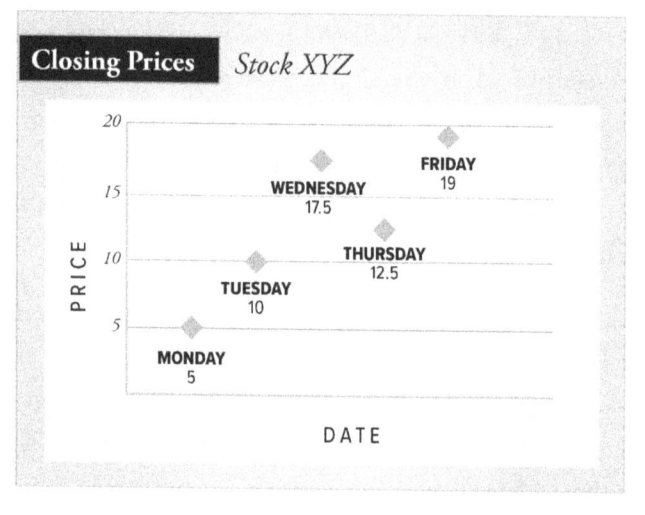

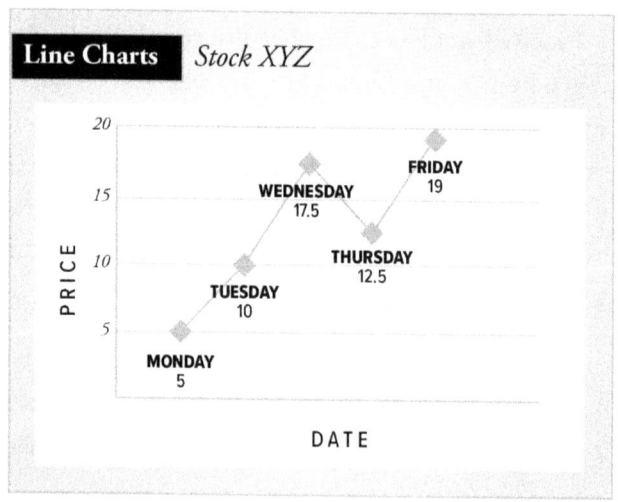

**Closing Prices** *Stock XYZ*

- MONDAY 5
- TUESDAY 10
- WEDNESDAY 17.5
- THURSDAY 12.5
- FRIDAY 19

**Line Charts** *Stock XYZ*

- MONDAY 5
- TUESDAY 10
- WEDNESDAY 17.5
- THURSDAY 12.5
- FRIDAY 19

A **bar chart** gives you more information, including the opening price, closing price, and high and low of the day. With a bar chart, the opening price is denoted by a slash sticking out to the left, while the middle vertical line represents the high and low of the day. The closing price is denoted by a slash sticking out on the right side.

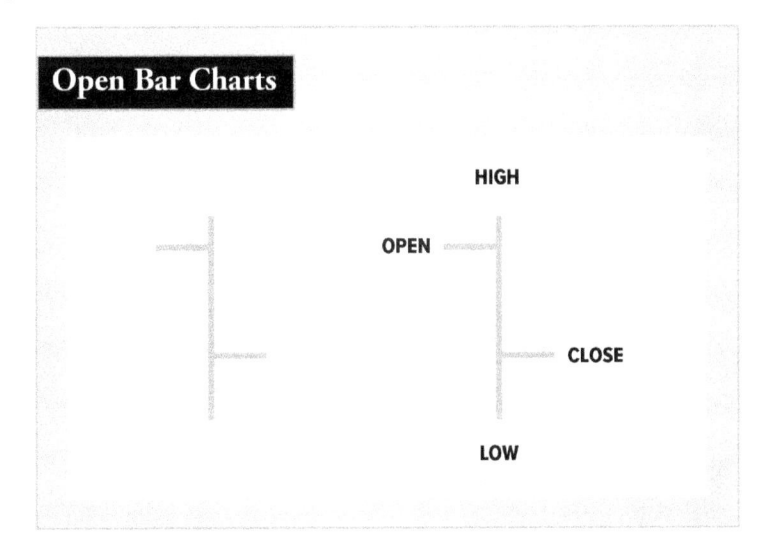

**Open Bar Charts**

```
                    HIGH
              OPEN ─┤
                    │
                    ├─ CLOSE
                    │
                    LOW
```

A **candlestick chart**, like a bar chart, gives you a little more information about how the stock behaved—but makes it easier to visualize, in my opinion. It shows you where the stock opened and closed as well as some of the activity that happened throughout the day. You can see if the stock opened lower, ran up, and then closed higher, or if the stock opened higher, then sold off, and closed lower. You can see where the high and low of the day are. It provides more information and paints a better picture. Was there a strong rally and lots of buying? Was it a bearish day with lots of selling? With a candlestick chart you really can get a good picture of how the stock performed for the day and draw better conclusions about where the stock may be headed next.

This information is crucial for determining if a trend might be ending, if it's time to enter a new trade, take a small loss, or take a profit before a stock turns and goes in the wrong direction.

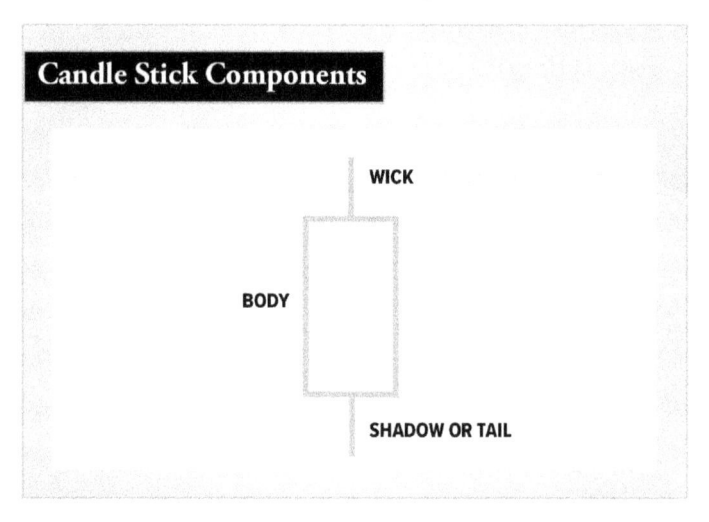

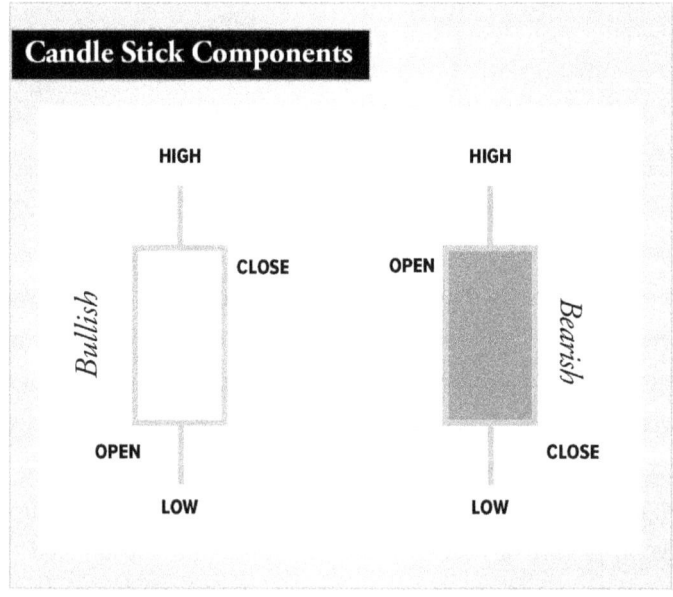

**Candle Stick Components**

- WICK
- BODY
- SHADOW OR TAIL

**Candle Stick Components**

*Bullish*: HIGH, CLOSE, OPEN, LOW

*Bearish*: HIGH, OPEN, CLOSE, LOW

## HOW DO I GET $1 MILLION INTO MY ACCOUNT?

When I first started trading, my thought was, "How do I make fifty dollars a week?" Once I accomplished that with only with $500 to start with, I looked at the math and saw that if I'd had $5K, then I could make $500 a week, and if I had $10K, I could make $1K a week. If I could make $1K a week at that time, with my living expenses being so low, I would be rich. So now my thought was, "How do I get ten thousand dollars into my trading account." After I became pretty good at reading stock charts, analyzing patterns, and using call and put options, I was able to scale my account to over $113K with the help of that student loan I mentioned earlier.

After eventually growing my trading account to $250K and then losing it all, I was no longer asking myself, "How do I get two hundred and fifty thousand dollars back into my account?" I'd already done that and knew it was possible. So, I began asking, "How do I get one million dollars into my account and what could I grow that to?"

At the time, I was still working to pay off my debts and get back on my feet. I already had a plan to live below my means, take advantage of a 401K, and invest my commission checks and the difference from living below my means back into the stock market.

I worked my way up the corporate ladder and was making six figures, but I wasn't putting the whole $100K into the market every year. I was living off about $50K a year and putting about $30K into the market and other investments. I did the math and discovered it would take me 10 years to get $300K into the market. So, now the new question was, how do I get $1 million in there in less than 35 years? Ideally in five to 10 years—that was the threshold I set for myself.

My plan for getting out of debt and into the market was working. I realized the more I earned in my job, the more I had available to put in the market. The more valuable an employee I was, the more I could make. Essentially, I became one of the best employees and top salespeople, not necessarily because I loved my job, but because the more I earned, the faster I could reach my goals of getting to a million-dollar account.

Once you have a gameplan—a starting and ending point for reaching your goals—you can start asking the question, "How do I speed it up?" I do this with everything in life. As long as I have the bare minimum gameplan, the next question is, "How do I speed this up?"

This was the same drive, determination, and thought process I applied to paying off my debt. When I looked at the numbers and how long it would take, I kept asking myself how to speed it up so I wouldn't be in debt for the rest of my life.

Similarly, when I looked at how long it would take for me to get a million dollars into my account at a minimum pace from working my job, I realized it would take 35 years. Then I asked myself, can I cut that time in half?

When it comes to reaching our financial goal, we often tell ourselves it will take us forever. That's what stops us from even trying. We are our own worst enemy when it comes to reaching for success. I'm always keen on finding out exactly how long it's going to take and then working backward to craft a game plan to speed it up from there. I believe it's important to look at every area of your life as a math equation, especially when it comes to making a sacrifice for your goals. It's important to remember that you're not downgrading your car or downsizing your house forever. You're doing it for a year or two or three while you regroup and get on your feet. As you get into a stronger financial situation, then you can buy it all back if you want to.

Having a strategic gameplan for my financial future was what got me through those tough times. And asking how I could speed it up was what helped me see the opportunities that were right in front of my face. I learned how to evaluate a Fortune 50 company from the inside by working for one, worked my way up to earn more so that I would have more to invest, and did things like take advantage of tuition reimbursement. When I told people I was going to school to finish my degree, some would say, "Getting a degree will take forever." But when you break it down, it's really only like five years, and you can speed that up by taking summer classes and night classes.

## TAKING CONTROL OF MY FUTURE

Toward the end of my time in corporate America, I thought about how keeping my job was blocking someone else's blessing. I was holding down a job I didn't even need anymore. By this time, I was—for the most part—out of debt, investing again, and had a business on the side that outproduced my W-2 income. There were people in the pipeline at work for whom making $100K a year would be life changing. I was making so much more outside of work that I had to free up that spot for someone who really needed it.

It was a moment in my life where, once again, I had to overcome fear and greed. I had to overcome the fear of wondering if I could make it outside of corporate America. The fear of having to pay my own health insurance. The fear that it might not last this time. The fear of "what if I'm not good enough." I also had to overcome the greed of trying to hold onto the job, the stock market, and the new side business.

I would ask myself things like: Who am I not to go after my dreams? Who better than me to be a full-time stock and options trader? Who, if not me, is going to teach the world these stock market lessons I learned?

Part of stepping out on your own as a stock market coach is understanding what it takes to run a business full-time. And part of being a full-time investor and entrepreneur is mastering fear and greed. When I left my job at Comcast, I made sure I was completely out of consumer debt, had fully paid off my student loans, and had six months of living expenses set aside. The stock market doesn't care what my expenses are. It's going to do what it's going to do regardless of if rent or a mortgage payment is due. The stock market doesn't operate on a "I need to cut you a check in two weeks" schedule.

Many people say they want to be a full-time trader. I believe that's possible for anyone who has a solid plan and discipline. The market will not pay you like clockwork every two weeks, and you shouldn't put that type of pressure on your trading and the stock market to perform every two weeks. You can remove that pressure by having low to no monthly bills and always having six months of living expenses saved. That way, you can sit through a few bad months or quarters of trades or not trading at all, waiting for the right opportunity without the pressure of, "If I don't make any money, I'll lose my house or get a ding on my credit score."

**CHAPTER 5: TAKEAWAYS**

- The stock market is not a scam.
- Money is all around us, you just have to think outside of the box to get it.
- Different types of stock charts give you different information in trading.
- Having a game plan is better than no game plan at all.

CHAPTER 6

# The Stock Market Doesn't Care That Rent Is Due Next Week

**L**ooking back on trades that went wrong and my experience of losing everything, I really tried to look internally and ask myself, "Why was I taking trades that were so high risk? When I took a loss, what made me feel like I needed to get my money back quickly?" Part of it was fear and greed. Greed being, "I want to make *this* much money. I want to pay cash for this condo. I'm not satisfied being up one hundred thousand dollars." I wanted to be up the entire $500K cost of the condo. Fear came with not wanting to miss out on a big trade. That fear changed into, "If I don't make enough money, I'll lose this lifestyle." I also became fearful that I couldn't make good decisions in the stock market and believed that no matter what, I would lose.

As I analyzed that fear and greed, it really came down to wanting to make a certain amount of money in a certain amount of time. I realized that I took one trade because I wanted to make $500K in a certain month to pay for the condo. I took another trade because I wanted to make back $75K in a certain amount of time because I wanted to see the money I had lost in my account again—immediately. I was trying to force my will on the market.

As I've said before, the stock market doesn't care what your plans are or what you want. It's going to do what it's going to do regardless of what you have planned for the money or your time frame for using that money if you make it.

Once you realize that the stock market doesn't care, it's your responsibility not to force your will on the market. You can't sit there thinking, "I'm going to make the market do this." You can't make it do anything. The best thing you can do is put yourself in a position where you don't need a specific amount of money in a specific amount of time. Then, when the stock market does give you an opportunity to enter and exit a low-risk, high-reward trade with profit, you're aware and prepared to take advantage of it.

## YOU CAN'T FORCE YOUR WILL ON THE MARKET

When people tell me, "I want to quit my job and be a trader," or "I want to use the stock market to fund some big purchase," or "How long do you think it'll take me to get good enough at this that I can quit my job?"—they're asking the wrong questions. The real question is, "How can I minimize my bills, living expenses, and debt so I don't need the market to do anything? How do I set myself up so I can wait for the predictable, repeatable patterns, and wait for the low risk, high returns without worrying about needing the money to pay bills by a certain date?"

Is it possible to make $100K in the market? Yes. But you don't know if you're going to make $8K a month for 12 months or if in month six you're going to make $50K and then in month 11 you'll make another $50K. The market is going to give it to you when it's going to give it to you and how it wants to give to you—if at all. Making money in the stock market is not going to be as easy and consistent as when you work a job and get a biweekly paycheck.

You have to be able to cover those bills until the market gives you a predictable, repeatable pattern to capitalize on—that may not be every two weeks or even in 30 days. You must also have enough trading capital to withstand losing money while remaining able to pull money out to pay your bills and still have money left over to trade.

I've had trades where I was down $20K. I came back and made $60K but it wasn't in the time frame I expected. If I had to sell that trade and take the $20K loss and still send $5K out for bills, that would be a painful experience if I couldn't wait for the market to turn around and do what I eventually thought it was going to do.

Yes, you must have the ability to spot the predictable, repeatable patterns when they're happening and then wait for them to play out the way you think they're going to play out. You must also ask yourself whether you have enough money to pay your bills and still live to trade another day if it doesn't play out. You have to weather all those different storms and environments. When you're a full-time trader, none of those environments are good for someone who has to worry about deadlines for paying bills or worry about losing the roof over their head if they don't make a certain amount from the stock market.

I made better trades and kept my stress and anxiety lower when I put myself in a financial position where I knew, "I don't need the stock market to do anything." I had no expectations. I believed stocks and the market were going up but whether they did or didn't had no impact on whether or not the lights would get turned off or if I could live in my house.

## MASTERING FEAR AND GREED

When you have expectations of the stock market that are tied to specific dates and specific amounts of money, you're really stirring up the fear and greed pot. You're fearful if it doesn't move up. You think, "How am I going to pay this bill?" Then if it does go up, it turns to greed. "How much higher can it go? I can't wait to buy that car, or that house, or go on that vacation with my profits."

Having specific dollar amounts or time expectations in the stock market is a recipe for disaster. Your expectations will have you staying in a trade longer than you should if you're winning, not appreciating the profit you have and, in most cases, leading you to giving all your profit back. If the stock is going against you, expecting that the stock will turn around will have you staying in a losing trade longer when you should be taking a small loss quickly. When you have expectations, fear and greed cloud your judgment and can cause you to not look at the stock market objectively.

In fact, if you're going to have expectations in the stock market, you should expect not to make money for six months or at least be prepared not to. There are events and times in the stock market when you might not want to trade or invest at all. There could be news of war or inflation that cause companies to have a bad quarter or two. Companies report earnings four times a year—every quarter, or three months. You might not want to trade over earnings due to the high volatility and unusual movement a stock can make during earnings announcements. You might want to take time off during the fourth quarter to enjoy the holidays and travel. So, there could be months where there is no real trading activity going on in your account.

Although you should hope for the best, you also need to plan for worst-case scenarios. If you have a bad month or two or three, you might need to pivot and get a job or a side hustle. Having six months of living expenses gives you a cushion to interview, get hired, trained, and get a paycheck. If you have a plan in place so your bills are covered for those remaining three months, it allows you to sleep better at night without worrying about getting behind or being afraid of losing your car or house.

Six months is a good run rate to allow you to breathe. Even if you don't trade for a month or two, you still have four months to make your next trade with your bills covered, so you're also able to be patient for two months and wait for the right setups. If you're in the right trade setup, you may need to wait two or three months for the trade to mature and play out. Hopefully, you can see how important having a six-month cushion is to trading full-time. If you can reduce your expenses and have no debt, it gives you that much more mental freedom when you're trading.

## MAKE YOUR MONEY A SECOND YOU

When I started studying wealth and wealthy people, I noticed two common threads—one, they had their money working hard for them, and two, they had multiple income streams. The stock market is one stream but ideally it shouldn't be your only stream. People say to me, "You do this full-time. How can I do that? How long did it take you?" The reality is it took me 10 to 20 years to get here. I'm giving you the blueprint to get here in five years. The first thing I did was reduce my expenses and then go to work on creating a secondary stream of income. For me that was the stock market. I eventually created more streams of income to help maintain the big picture of not going back to work full-time but staying full-time as a trader.

I make money from my YouTube channel, The Brown Report, and my stock market education company, Power Trades University, just to name a few. I have about seven streams of income and things to fall back on, so I will never need to get a conventional job again unless I really wanted to. I have my real estate license if I ever have to get out there and hustle in sales to make some money. I have my college degree and work experience in my back pocket if I ever have to go get a high-paying job. Plus, everything I own for the most part is paid off and I have no consumer debt.

Regardless of how many other streams of income you have, the stock market should definitely be one of them. Your money can work harder for you than you can for it. The stock market can make money faster than you can sell houses or faster than you can go back to school and get a degree or climb the corporate ladder. The beauty of the stock market is that while you work your full-time job, your money can be working a second shift from 9:30 a.m. to 4 p.m.—the market hours—creating a second stream of income immediately without requiring much of your time or physical labor.

Instead of trying to quit your job to trade full-time, use your job to provide you with hard-earned money that you can employ in the stock market, making you some smart-earned money. Reduce your expenses so every dollar above what you need to live on from your W-2 can go into a system where it doesn't get tired, ask for vacations or time off, catch COVID-19, or need time off for grievance. Your money works—and when you are a good manager of it, your money goes out and recruits more green employees.

Money is like a robot. It has no thoughts, emotions, or will of its own. It doesn't talk back or complain. It's the perfect thing to put to work as a second you—or a better second you. It doesn't get sick or need to sleep, and it can work all day long without taking breaks. This is the game the wealthy play. This is how they get paid for 48 or 72 hours or more without physically working for it. The wealthy usually have money and business systems working for them. If you can't build a business system, the stock market allows you to buy into some of the best business systems and come along for the profit ride.

If you're working 9 a.m. to 5 p.m. and your money is also working for you 9:30 a.m. to 4 p.m., it's the equivalent of working 16 hours a day or two full-time shifts a day. That's where you start to get leverage—the same type of leverage the wealthy use to get rich: time leverage, people leverage, and money leverage.

In the stock market, you get to leverage all three. Let me explain. Not everyone can start a business and hire employees for the people leverage. Not everyone has the time nor the desire to work two jobs. And we all only have 24 hours in a day. However, with the stock market you can leverage time because your money is working for you. You get to leverage people because someone else is running the companies you're investing in and managing the employees while you get the benefit of their genius business ideas and inventions.

Think about it like this: can you build a better iPhone than Apple or a better social media platform than Facebook or a better highspeed, global food-delivery system than McDonald's? No. Then what better way to profit off those successful companies than to buy the stock and tag along with all the employees those companies have and all the work they do. You can bypass all the headache of trying to start a competing business and join competent leaders of cutting-edge companies by putting your money with them and investing in the stock or controlling the stock with options. That's people and business leverage at its finest.

How long would it take you—staying up at night—to learn to code and build the next social media platform while working your full-time job? How long to learn how to start a business, hire people, market and sell your product, file for patents, and build retail distribution globally? A long, long time if you ever get there at all.

As an alternative, you could look at the stocks of companies like Apple and McDonald's and say, "Okay, I'll buy some shares and let them figure out the rest." I'll tag along for the ride and use their engineers, employees, and management team. After all, publicly traded companies ultimately work for the shareholders.

If you don't want to learn how to start a business, manage a company, hire people, fire people, and all that, you can buy shares of the stock and go along for the ride. When you own shares, you own a stake in the company. They have to report their earnings and how the company is doing quarterly to their shareholders. Their CEOs have to hold press conferences to announce what they're doing and why. If you own shares, depending on what kind of shares they are, you can even vote on certain important decisions regarding the company. You get a say in the company by owning shares of the stock.

It's such a powerful position that I find it disrespectful when people enter the stock market and treat it like gambling when it's so much more than closing your eyes and throwing a dart to pick a stock. You actually get to become an owner of some of the most powerful companies in the world. All of this is made possible by having your money become a second you by investing it in this powerful machine called the stock market.

## NEWCOMER MISTAKES IN THE MARKET

Hopefully now you can see you see the power of having your money work for you in the stock market. Before getting started, there are some common mistakes that I see new traders and investors often make. Let's talk about them.

**Common mistake number one** is when new investors and traders think they can do it all on their own. They think, "I'm going to do this my way and if I lose my money, I'll get coaching then. I'll take a course then." Sadly, all too often, I get emails from those first-timers that say, "I blew up my account. I should have taken your course or gotten some coaching. When I rebuild my account, I'm going to join you and get the right support and knowledge." People don't do this in any other area of life, but for some reason they do it in the stock market. We don't jump into a car for the first time and start driving it without driver training or learning what road signs and traffic lights mean, but in the stock market we try to figure it out ourselves. Usually, the type of people who do that end up in a stock market accident with a total loss.

**Common mistake number two** is that new traders and investors don't practice. They're so excited to get started and make real money that they come into the industry and forget they can also lose money. They don't take the time to practice and sometimes don't even know how to get out of a trade they've entered—they jump in without knowing how to stop the bleeding on a losing trade. Today, you can practice in a virtual account or simulated real account that allows you to get a feel for the platform and learn how to enter and exit trades with virtual profit and loss to test how good your investment and trading theory is.

**Common mistake number three** is buying a well-known stock without looking at the chart or doing any research. It's easy to think, Apple (AAPL) is releasing a new iPhone, or Google (GOOGL) owns YouTube, that's doing well, or Facebook (META) launched a new app—I'll buy their stock and surely it will go up. But let's not forget that on September 1, 2021, Facebook fell from $384 a share and didn't stop falling until it dropped to $88 a share on November 4, 2022.[4] There are countless other examples that show there are bad times to buy a so-called good stock. Lawsuits, poor earnings, scandals, and war are all things that can make even a good stock drop like a rock. Just because a company is well-known doesn't mean you can go in blind—new and

---

4 "Meta Platforms, Inc. (META) Sep. 1, 2021–Nov. 30, 2022," Yahoo! Finance, accessed May 8, 2024, https://finance.yahoo.com/quote/META/history/?period1=1630454400&period2=1669766400.

experienced investors and traders still need to do their homework even if they're familiar with a company or use their products.

When new traders and investors jump in without practice, thinking they can do it all on their own, they're approaching the market from a place of fear of missing out and greed—wanting to dive in and make a lot of money so they can spend it and live large , without first investing some of that money in education.

**Common mistake number four** is not taking into account the risk versus reward ratio of a trade. Many new traders walk into every trade looking only at the upside—how much money they can make—and not calculating the risk and taking into account how much they can lose or whether a trade fits their risk profile. This approach is driven by fear and greed. Greedy new traders think every trade is going to the moon and they fear missing out on the ride up.

I teach the traders who participate in my stock market education platform, Power Trades University, to look for a 1:3 risk versus reward ratio. For every dollar you risk, you need to have the potential to make at least $3. You can't remove risk completely but if you're going to take a calculated risk, you want the upside to be worth three times what you could potentially lose. In terms of money, I'm taking about taking a risk where you're putting up $100 for the potential of bringing $400 back, which equates to $300 profit. That's a good risk versus reward ratio.

Think about it. This goes back to the "running yellow lights" concept I talked about earlier. If you make it through the light, you get to your destination a few seconds faster. If you don't, you could kill yourself or the driver of another car. That's a bad risk versus reward ratio, yet many people take that trade every day, risking their lives for such a little reward. As applied to the stock market, your trading account is your life. You don't want to blow up your trading account—especially not for very little reward potential. You want to take smarter, more calculated risks with better risk versus reward ratios.

## HAVE A GAME PLAN

Investing is all about having a game plan. That game plan—be it long-term investing where you're holding stock for longer than a year, day trading where you're in and out of stocks in the same day, swing trading (trying to profit off short-term price patterns in 90 days or less), or any other type of trading—should be to manage risk for reward. Let's say you have $5. It's okay to risk $1 to make $3 because if you lose the $1, you still have $4 left. With $4 left, if you risk $1 again to make $3 and the trade works in your favor, you now have $7.00 to invest. Essentially you can be wrong one or two times in a row and be right once—you'll still be profitable and net positive.

Let's say you have $5 to invest and you risk $1 and lose it, then risk $1 again and lose it, then risk $1 again and lose it, you still have $2 left. If you make the $3 back on the fourth trade, then you're at least back to breaking even. You want to have the opportunity to be wrong and still live to trade another day. You can do that comfortably with a 1:3 risk versus reward ratio.

If you're taking a 1:1 risk versus reward, then you're risking a dollar to make a dollar. If you risk your only $500 to make $500 and lose it all, then that's it, game over.

If you are going to take 1 to 1 or 50/50 bets, then you might as well go to the casino.

How many times can you lose 50% or 100% of your account and still live to trade another day? It's simple math. If you lose 100%, you can only do that once. If you lose 50%, you can only do that twice. If you're at a 1:3 risk versus reward, you can do those three or four times and still be okay. Approaching the stock market with the 1:3 risk versus reward mindset allows you to start playing the game like a true money manager rather than one of those traders who gamble and blow up their account.

Now let's talk about what kind of time frame you'll need to commit to the stock market to see a major financial change in your life and movement toward your life's major goals. Many people come into the stock market expecting instant results—if they don't see life-changing money in six months to a year, they're ready to quit. And yet, we commit to spending a minimum of four years in college to get a piece of paper so we can come out hopefully making $50K to $100K a year and we're willing to go $50K into debt to get that degree.

**What if in four to five years committed to this industry, you could become a millionaire? That's what I'm going to show you if you have the patience to learn, practice, and use a 1:3 risk versus reward ratio with predictable, repeatable patterns. It's possible to become a millionaire in the stock market in about the same amount of time it takes to get a college degree.**

**CHAPTER 6: TAKEAWAYS**

- The stock market doesn't care that your rent is due or that bills need to be paid.
- The market is going to move on its own time frame—you can't force it.
- You have the power to make your money work for you like the wealthy do.
- Avoid the most common mistakes new traders make: going into investing alone, not practicing before putting real money down, buying well-known stocks without looking at the chart, and quitting their day job to trade stocks full-time without a real game plan.
- You want to be able to be wrong and still be profitable. Know your "I'm Wrong" level and when it's time to get out of a trade.

CHAPTER 7

# The Five-Year Millionaire Plan

I didn't set out on my financial journey with the goal of being a millionaire in mind, though it was something I would say jokingly like most people—"Someday, I want to become a millionaire." I really wanted to be financially free. I remember sitting down and making a list of everything I wanted in life and estimating what each thing on my list would cost me annually. This is an exercise I think everyone should try because it provided me with clarity that changed my life. I made a vision board, and I wrote about the things I wanted to have in my life eventually—a wife, three kids, private school tuition for the kids, vacations, how much I wanted to spend on those vacations, the cars I wanted to drive, the house I wanted to live in, etc. I wrote down everything and mapped it out. And I didn't stop there. I researched the costs and put real numbers to all of it—how much my dream car, cost at the time, and how much a house on a lake cost.

I pushed away all thoughts of "I'll never be able to afford this," or "This isn't realistic, or it will take forever and probably will never happen at all." The point of the vision board wasn't to create goals for what I could achieve based on my situation at that time. The point was to give myself permission to be honest with what I really wanted in life and then give myself the creative space to figure out how to chart a path to get there and go after it if I chose to. I determined what it would take to get there based on my future potential if I learned, earned, and grew personally and professionally.

The number I came up with to live my dream lifestyle was an annual income of $500K. This number included what I had researched for how much all the things on my vision board would cost plus extra for investing and saving. That was when I realized for the first time that I didn't need to become a millionaire to live my dream lifestyle.

Lots of people blindly wish to be millionaires. When you ask them why, they say things like, "Well, I'll be able to travel, live in this house, and drive that car." Many of them don't realize that perhaps their dream life doesn't require making a million dollars. I was one of those people. It was a big moment for me to understand that I could get my dream life for $500K—"half off" what I thought I'd needed to earn. That also meant I didn't need to put in so much effort or pressure on myself to become a millionaire. I only needed to put in the effort of "half a millionaire." Instead of working double hard for double the amount of money needed for my dream life, as many people do, I realized it wasn't nearly as expensive as I thought it would be. Getting to half a million would pretty much cover everything and give me some cushion. I'd have a pretty good life and it was a lot more realistic to me at the time than reaching for a million.

As I was working my way up the corporate ladder, trading, and building my business on the side, my thinking was that I could use all three of those money-making opportunities to get to half a million—and I eventually did.

I had been earning over half of million dollars from my investments, job, and business for a few years, but I never thought about the fact that I had made more than a million dollars total or that I might even be a net-worth millionaire. Basically, in my mind, if I wasn't earning $1 million in one calendar year, I didn't count it. So, when I eventually made over a million dollars in one year, I thought, "Wow, I did it. I finally made it." Yet when I logged in to check my account, I saw that I was already a net-worth millionaire. I wasn't paying attention to my net worth because I was caught up in the "I need to make a million dollars in one year" mindset. I didn't realize how I had consistently been chipping away at the proverbial millionaire status and that, technically, I was already a millionaire based on my net worth.

My life had already changed so much by the time I made $500K in one year that making $1 million in one year didn't really change much in my lifestyle. My family had already moved into our dream house. I was already driving my dream cars. When I realized I'd hit that new financial goal, it didn't really mean anything—my life wasn't going to change that much making $1 million. I wasn't going to buy a bigger house or a different car. What it did give me was curiosity as to whether it was a one-time thing. Was it a fluke? Did I get lucky? Can I do it again? But after earning $1 million a second year in a row, it was clear that it wasn't luck and that I now knew what it took to earn that kind of money.

When I look at the time frame from deciding that I wanted to earn a million dollars and eventually becoming a millionaire, it was roughly five years. That's how I came up with the idea of the Five-Year Millionaire. I started researching how I could help others get there with or without a side hustle or starting their own business—with or without having a lot of money to invest. I wanted to help people with less than $5K to invest, which is where I started. Most people can scrape together a couple thousand dollars by saving their tax returns and a side hustle like driving Uber or Lyft. I was excited because it meant I could help the masses—wherever they are—and share a roadmap for becoming a millionaire.

When I was a kid, I got tired of looking to strangers—usually white strangers—to tell me the secret of wealth. Growing up in Detroit, we really didn't know anyone who amassed true wealth or was a millionaire—and if anyone in my family or our circle *were* millionaires, they didn't want anyone to know, including us kids. We were always looking for someone to "share the secret" and open the door for us kids or point us in the right direction. Outside of becoming a rapper in the music industry or playing sports, there were no clear opportunities to get us out of the neighborhood and into the millionaire lifestyle. I wanted to get to a place where I didn't need to seek out random strangers for advice. I wanted to get to a point where I knew what it took and what to do. I wanted to become the mentor and the source, a person who others could come to—to find out how I did it.

I thought about all this in terms of my kids, too. If they wanted to make that kind of money and know what it takes to make $1 million, honestly, I didn't want to tell them to go talk to someone else's dad. I want them to be able to get the answers right at home. I can tell them what it takes, my mindset, the sacrifices I made, and what I went through. I wanted to be in that power position with that knowledge for myself and as a resource for my children, my friends, and my family.

## 60 TRADES AND 10%

I learned that becoming a millionaire was a math equation. What do I have to do? How many times do I have to do it? And for how long? In the stock market, that equation is 60 trades at a 10% profit or one trade a month that produces a 10% profit for five years or several trades a month that add up to a 10% return a month for five years, assuming you start with a $4,000 investment account.

My life changed the most between making $300K and $500K. My lifestyle didn't change much when I started making over $500K. Between $300K and $500K, I was able to afford what I wanted and live the life I had drawn out on my vision board. At that level, there's not much more you need or can't already afford. You can only drive one or two cars, reasonably. You can only really live in one house at a time. Unless you make the jump from millionaire to multimillionaire, your life isn't going to change all that much after $500K. I wasn't expecting that. I think partially it's because the next jump in luxury lifestyle is so high, meaning you're looking at private jets and $10 million homes which require a whole other level of wealth.

Once I hit the millionaire benchmark, we didn't move. We didn't buy a second home, and we didn't upgrade our cars once again. The message I want people to take away from this is that I didn't feel some big life change because my life had been changing incrementally on my way to becoming a millionaire. There was no big "Aha!" moment with champagne corks popping and a party to celebrate my becoming a millionaire.

As your earnings grow incrementally from $100K to the $300k or $400K and $500K level, your lifestyle and the things you're able to afford jump drastically compared to when your earnings increased from $50K to $100K. But the difference between $100K and $500K is more significant in terms of lifestyle than $500K to $1 million. You can already afford what you want. You're already controlling your time and can pay off your cars, house, and any debt in a reasonable timeframe.

That was the track my family and I were on. We paid off the house in two years after a $411K profitable trade. I didn't need to make a million to make that happen while still being able to afford the rest of our life. When I did make a million later that year it was like, "We're already living that life." It was kind of anti-climactic because when you make that kind of life-changing money, the front end of your life doesn't change much, but you get to clean up the back end of your life—the part that nobody sees, like paying off your house and growing your retirement accounts. People saw I lived in a nice house, but paying it off in two years wasn't as exciting as first buying it and moving in—for me or for those on the outside looking in. They only saw that I bought it and lived in it. Same thing when I paid off the cars. To the outside world, nothing changed—but on the books, in my credit report, and for my mental health, things changed because I didn't have debt.

The problem with buying things with debt financed by credit is that you get to enjoy now what you haven't fully worked or paid for. In essence, you pull forward the enjoyment but delay the non-fun process of working hard and then giving up the money to pay for the items. Those back-end accomplishments aren't as sexy as the front-end pleasure. Paying off your house isn't nearly as exciting as the day you get your keys to move in. Maybe you'll take a picture of your spouse and yourself outside your brand-new front door the day you move in to share with friends and family. You probably won't take a picture of your mortgage statement when the last payment is made to share with everyone, although more people probably should.

When you move in it's a feeling of, "Whoa, we live here, wow!" You've already pulled forward that joy when you financed the house. You financed your future joy.

For me, something interesting happened once I got to a million—I kind of transitioned into a mental zone where it wasn't about making more millions but about not wanting to lose the million. I didn't want to spend it all because it took a lot to get there. I didn't know if I'd make a million every year in the market or from business. So, as a Five-Year Millionaire, you're not going to take five years to get to a million and then blow it all in one year—at least you shouldn't. That's how irresponsible lottery winners, artists, and athletes go broke.

Think of it like this. Just because you make a million dollars doesn't mean you have a million to spend. You have $100K to $200K to spend with the other $800K being used to generate cash flow—and let's not forget about paying taxes. I hope you didn't think all that money is yours to keep tax-free.

It's important to pace yourself on your way to making a million but also to pace your expectations once you get there. The money can go really quickly, and you have to preserve it. You have to see how you can protect it and grow it to the next two, three, or four million.

I made $411K in a trade and I immediately paid off my house. That money was gone, but not really, because I still had access to it through a HELOC (home equity line of credit) if I needed it. That's how becoming a Five-Year Millionaire is different from being a lottery millionaire. You've conditioned yourself over those five years to not only make a million but also to think like a millionaire, to delay gratification, to commit yourself for a longer period of time to learn a skill that will last you a lifetime. Because you're making money along the way, you're not pulling it out and spending it—you're using it to grow to that million. If you do pull some of it out, you're not worried that this is a one-hit wonder like winning the Powerball. You don't have to hope and pray that the lottery will hit again. You now have a skill and discipline and know how to print money legally from the stock market.

You can tell yourself that no matter what happens in your life, even if you lose everything, you can take $4K and start over and work toward becoming a millionaire again in five years. There's power in knowing you can do that. That's what makes me feel so calm and confident that I'll never be broke. Five-Year Millionaire is not just about making a million dollars. It's about becoming a millionaire as a person and in your mindset and habits.

I'm a millionaire even if I'm flat broke because I see money, investing, businesses, and companies differently. I see raising capital to get in the market differently. I've already made a million dollars, so I know if I did it once, I can do it again. If life ever knocks me down, I know how to get on my feet and back on the millionaire track. If I'm down, I know it's only a matter of time before I return to millionaire status—if I choose to put in the work.

That's part of what becoming a Five-Year Millionaire is about. If you can embrace the process of identifying patterns in stock charts, determining the best time to buy and sell, taking a 1:3 risk versus reward ratio, and mastering fear and greed—and if you can do that for a five-year period—your life can completely change. And I'm not just talking about a financial life change.

If you can stay focused and grow your account for five years, you'll have invested through one presidential election, changing interest rates, and economic conditions. You'll have the skills and qualifications to become a millionaire in almost any market conditions because, for the most part, in five years you'll have seen and experienced it all.

You'll have seen different aspects of the economy playing out. If you can stay focused and invested during five years and survive while making 60 trades at a 10% return, you'll have earned the crown of the Five-Year Millionaire. You'll have the skillset, knowledge, and experience to restart the process. No matter what happens to you in life, you know how to become a millionaire in five years. That's the power in what we're teaching and in starting your Five-Year Millionaire journey.

## GROW WITH YOUR MONEY

Going to college or a university for four or five years is a gameplan to make $50K to $100K and, depending on your life circumstances, go into debt to do it. That's not a bad thing. I went to school for my degree, and it helped me raise the floor of what a company would be willing to pay me. It ensured I wouldn't end up living at my mom's again if I ever lost all my investments or my business and had to go find a job.

But going to school isn't a gameplan for becoming a millionaire—

though it can be part of the plan. You need to carve out your own gameplan for that goal. The Five-Year Millionaire gameplan inside my platform, Power Trades University, is where you can learn valuable skills—like trading stocks and options—and then use those skills to get you on the fast track to becoming a millionaire without going deep into debt. Much like a college degree, once you earn the paper, it's yours to keep. The knowledge can be passed down to your children and around to friends and family members.

Five years is about the time it takes to master the disciplines of investing and spending and learn impulse control with respect to managing finances—not blowing your money each time you get a big return, but re-investing and delaying gratification for the ultimate pay day.

There's a saying I love: "It would be a shame if your money grew but you didn't." A lot of people who win big money—lottery winnings, casino winnings, or large inheritances—see their money grow quickly, but don't grow quickly enough themselves with it. They have the same spending habits that led them to be broke, and the money vanishes almost as quickly as it came, with no way of getting it back.

The Five-Year Millionaire plan has built-in personal development components that teach you to grow as your money grows. On this Five-Year Millionaire journey, you have to learn how to overcome fear and greed, exercise discipline and patience, and commit to and execute a plan. At times it can be tempting to want to rush the process and speed things up. Recently, a member of the program—I'll call him Jimmy—decided to leave. We were two months ahead of schedule on our Five-Year Millionaire plan because we'd found some extra-profitable trades. Jimmy left because he wanted to trade more often and more aggressively or wanted our team to send him more trades more often—and quite possibly with more risk.

In my view, as someone experienced in this industry, what that usually equates to is that Jimmy is going to put more money into riskier trades than he needs to. He's going to start to ignore the process we've worked on and blow up his account. It's tough but not impossible to find one trade a month that delivers 10% profit. True, there are times when we find two or three, but we don't take every trade and every trade is not always a winner.

When Jimmy trades more often, it's like saying, "I can find five to ten of these trades a month and I'll be right on most of them." The odds are not in his favor. The reality is getting rich is easy if you follow a simple plan—the problem is people don't like to or have the patience to follow a simple plan. They get bored. The plan is simple enough: 60 trades at a 10% return (ideally one a month) for five years.

I really hope Jimmy comes back in a year or two and tells me he became a millionaire faster. More often than not, when people who are already doing well decide to trade more aggressively and then start putting too much at risk or doing too many trades, they end up losing all their money. They go from trading monthly to weekly to daily, and then greed starts to kick in, they no longer stick with the plan, and they get further off the path of the original process.

I get emails from these people that usually goes something like this: "I was doing really well when I was with you guys in the Five-Year Millionaire Program." Then comes the "but," there's always a "but." "But then I stopped following the process, I started getting greedy..." And it usually ends with, "But then I took too many risky trades, lost money, and now my account is at zero and I have to start over."

It's possible to compress the five-year plan by trying for two trades a month at 10%. You could become a millionaire in two years. The five-year goal is already a little on the aggressive side, so trying to compress the time puts you in a position where you have to find more trades faster and closer together and be right on all of them. This puts you in a place where the odds are less in your favor.

It's possible to find that 10% return once a month if you know what you're looking for. It's less likely you'll find two or four on a consistent basis and get in and out at all the right times.

You never know 100% that a trade is going to work out. Think of your money like soldiers. You send your soldiers out to war and hope they return home. Maybe they'll bring some captured green soldiers (aka more money) with them—at least that's the plan.

Your money is the same—going out to war against poverty, war against broke-ness. You send your troops into the market and hope they come back with more little green guys. But there's no guarantee they'll come back home. Your troops could get captured. You don't want to over-confidently send your money out to war 5 to 10 times a month assuming it will always be an easy mission and your money will come back home.

Now in terms of your own life, how often would you be willing to go to the front lines of a war—especially if you've already gone out once and survived to come home. You survived World War I and II, but how many more times are you going to get in the line of fire? Are you going to go to war every week or several times a week to speed things up, or only go to war when you see a strategic advantage and a high probability you'll win? It's the same with your money and investing in the stock market. You only want to send your money-soldiers out to war when you see a strategic advantage or when there's a high probability they'll come back home with more soldiers.

There are very few scenarios where you look at war—or in this case investing—like it's a walk in the park. There are a lot more scenarios where every money mission has some element of risk that can't be diminished. You only want to send your troops out when the opportunity is right and you have a strategy.

You're not going to hit a big trade every day or even every week. People who think that every day is a good day to strike are ignoring the enemy choppers and the land mines. They might think five years is too slow, but they'll work 40 years for someone else and never get there, so what's the rush?

## YOUR MILLIONAIRE JOURNEY

There have been weeks when I made $43K in five days but I didn't get to that level overnight. Those kinds of profits could pay for a college degree without going into debt. Working toward that type of paydays and those types of opportunities is part of what the Five-Year Millionaire is about. Remember, you have to grow into it, not rush into it. You won't get there if everything has to be fast and quick. People who rush make simple, unnecessary mistakes. How many times can you have a $43K day? The moment you believe that every day needs to be a $43K day or believe you can effortlessly produce $43K profits every week is the beginning of the end. There's a good chance you're taking uncalculated risk, overlooking major landmines that can blow up your account, or simply sending your soldiers out to war too often. Sooner or later, they won't come back home.

The trades we look for are low risk, high reward, and they don't show up every day or every week.

If you can get an account started with $4K on your journey and learn how to grow that $4K investment while getting 10% returns once a month for five years or 60 trades, then you'll end up with roughly $1.2 million dollars. You can always get started with a smaller amount, like I did with my original $500. It might take longer than five years but that shouldn't discourage you from getting going.

| STARTING CAPITAL TRADES | Year 1 | | Year 2 | | Year 3 | | Year 4 | | Year 5 |
|---|---|---|---|---|---|---|---|---|---|
| JAN STARTING CAPITAL $4,000 | $4,400 | 1 | $13,809 | 13 | $43,339 | 25 | $136,016 | 37 | $426,876 |
| FEB | $4,480 | 2 | $15,190 | 14 | $47,673 | 26 | $149,617 | 38 | $469,563 |
| MARCH | $5,324 | 3 | $16,709 | 15 | $52,440 | 27 | $164,579 | 39 | $516,520 |
| APRIL | $5,856 | 4 | $18,380 | 16 | $57,684 | 28 | $181,037 | 40 | $568,172 |
| MAY | $6,442 | 5 | $20,218 | 17 | $63,452 | 29 | $199,141 | 41 | $624,989 |
| JUNE | $7,086 | 6 | $22,240 | 18 | $69,798 | 30 | $219,055 | 42 | $687,488 |
| JULY | $7,795 | 7 | $24,464 | 19 | $76,777 | 31 | $240,960 | 43 | $756,237 |
| AUG | $8,574 | 8 | $26,910 | 20 | $84,455 | 32 | $265,056 | 44 | $831,860 |
| SEPT | $9,432 | 9 | $29,601 | 21 | $92,901 | 33 | $291,562 | 45 | $915,046 |
| OCT | $10,375 | 10 | $32,561 | 22 | $102,191 | 34 | $320,718 | 46 | $1,006,551 |
| NOV | $11,412 | 11 | $35,817 | 23 | $112,410 | 35 | $352,790 | 47 | $1,107,206 |
| DEC | $12,554 | 12 | $39,399 | 24 | $123,651 | 36 | $388,069 | 48 | $1,217,927 |

Let's talk about learning how to grow your account. At Power Trades University, my team and I look for these types of trades for ourselves, then we share them with the community. Essentially, we do the research for you on which trades to look at that are ideally low-risk, high-reward and have the potential to return 10% a month. In the Five-Year Millionaire program, you get email and text alerts and either a video or written analysis for trades that meet our Power Trades criteria.

There's an old proverb that goes: "Give a man a fish and you feed him for a day, teach a man to fish and you feed him for a lifetime." I don't want to give you fish—I want to teach you how to fish. Then you can teach your family and friends how to fish and provide food—in this case financial food … money!—for years and generations to come.

I'm often asked what's the best way to learn and how long does it take? If you can dedicate at least two hours a week to learning and practicing, that's a great start. I have found one of the best ways to learn is by studying for a good hour and then practicing—or watching someone put into action—what I was studying for another hour. It's also important to ask questions about what you learned or , if you are confused, to get feedback from someone more experienced in the stock market game. That is how I structure the programs at Power Trades University, with the three Cs in mind: **Courses, Coaching**, and **Community**.

For the first "C" we have courses that you can follow at your own pace to learn the industry, language, and art of trading—a minimum of one hour a week is recommended. There's also a live component where you can watch me or one of the other coaches on the team apply what's taught in the courses—watch us find real trades in the real market.

The courses are designed so you understand the language of the market, have your account set up and ready to go—either on a practice or real account—and so you understand some of the big picture ideas and smaller details of trading. In that way, you'll know what to do—and understand what we're looking for—once you come to the live session and apply strategies. More specifically, within the courses you learn how to do fundamental research, read stock charts, determine the best time to buy and sell, and what a low-risk high-return trade looks like with a minimum 1:3 risk versus reward ratio.

Students have asked, "Should I study the courses and learn as much as possible before joining a live trading and research session?" It's best to go through the course and the live sessions together to learn how to apply what you've studied. It's kind of like burning the candle at both ends in a good way—when the two meet in the middle, you have a greater understanding of the process. I've seen people study and study and never pause to apply what they've learned. Then, by the time they face a real-life application, they've forgotten some of the earlier stuff they studied because they never put it into practice.

In the live sessions, we apply technical analysis to the charts and look at the overall market and individual stocks to determine if we're bullish or bearish and if we think the market or a stock is going up or down based on trend analysis. We look at the different options strategies we can use to minimize our risk and ideally generate a power return. We also set our "I'm Wrong" levels—where we'll get out if the trade goes against us—in these sessions. The community asks questions and discusses whether they want to be in on the trade and if it fits their individual trading plan. There's a community forum for sharing ideas with each other and getting feedback on other stocks that members may have found, and there's an all-around network with other traders.

Often, what prevents people from getting started on their millionaire journey is the perception that it's going to take a lot of time. The reality is, getting rich is not going to happen by accident and you're going to have to make the time. However, I realize that many people have a busy schedule like I've had, with school, my significant other, community activities, and now raising a family. I designed the courses so they can be consumed in bite-sized chunks the way I consumed information on my lunch breaks, in my car, and waiting in line for food. All the course modules are designed to be about 20 to 30 minutes, so you can consume the information in small pockets during your day. To ensure you know what you think you learned, we've built in quizzes at the end of each course and put together PDF cheat sheets for quick-reference access to the information reviewed in the modules.

Let's talk about the second "C" on your Five-Year Millionaire journey—coaching. The coaching happens live while looking at the real market. It's one thing to learn something in theory but another to watch how to implement it while real things are happening to make stocks move up or down.

Although all the sessions are live, they're recorded for watching on your own time if you can't make it for the live session. We provide a spreadsheet of all the stocks we found and discussed in the live session, the technical patterns we see setting up, the option plays, the ideal entry into the trade, the "I'm Wrong" level, and everything else you need to know to make an informed decision if you choose to practice trading those stocks and options strategies.

The third "C" is community. When I was trading in my early days, I so longed to find other traders to chat with—other people who understood the ups and downs and were looking at stocks on a regular basis. I wanted to know if they saw the same things I did. My cousin was the only trader I knew within my close circle of family and friends back then. It often felt like a lonely sport. That's why, when I built Power Trades University, it was imperative that we have a community aspect so our traders could network, share knowledge, fellowship with other traders, and talk around the clock about the stock market, stocks, and options.

But I didn't want to create just any old traders' community, I wanted to create a community of people who traded with somewhat the same methodology. I had been in Facebook groups and Reddit forums where you're thrown in with people who trade Bitcoin and FOREX (foreign exchange) with day traders, swing traders, penny stock traders, and commodity traders. It became confusing, convoluted, hard to find the right information, and harder to find people who traded in the same style. Furthermore, most of the people in those free forums and communities were compulsive stock gamblers—or at least that's how they behaved.

In Power Trades University, as of right now, the only way to get into the community and forums is to go through the coaching and courses that allow you to understand the methodology that we believe makes a successful trader.

1. Looking for predictable repeatable patterns.
2. Taking 1:3 minimum risk versus reward ratio trades.
3. Knowing your "I'm Wrong" level.

We don't attract a community of gamblers who go broke because they don't know when to quit. We want a community of educated risk managers who have a solid game plan.

On your journey to becoming a millionaire, it's not going to be a smooth ride, but I can guarantee it's going to be a lot smoother if you have the three Cs on your side: Courses, Coaching, Community.

**CHAPTER 7: TAKEAWAYS**

- Create a dream/vision board with everything you want in life.
- Determine the real cost of living your dream lifestyle.
- Develop a millionaire's mindset and habits.
- Remember that sending your money out to the stock market is like sending your soldiers out to war. Be sure you have a plan and a strategy, and the odds are in your favor.
- Understand the three Cs: Coaching, Courses, Community.

CHAPTER 8

# Protecting Your "Ass"ets

**On the journey to making** money in the stock market—and after accumulating some wealth—one of the big things most people worry about is how to protect what they've made. If you've come into the stock market game with a substantial amount of money, you worry about how not to lose it all. No one wants to lose their money or life savings. We've all heard the stories of "I tried something in the stock market and lost everything," or "I was doing really well, making a lot of money, then the market changed and before I knew it, I was down to zero."

Whether you're just getting started, are in the middle of your journey, or have already made it, you've got to protect your assets, which can be done in various ways: options, stop-loss triggers, diversification of investment strategies, and by understanding how to spot and avoid high-risk times to buy in the stock market.

## OPTIONS AS INSURANCE

One of my favorite ways to protect my assets in the stock market is to buy options as insurance in the same way that I would buy insurance for my car or home. Most people don't know they can do that or that it's even an option (pun intended). Just as you have insurance on your house to protect it from fire or other disastrous events, you can protect your investment account with put options that insure against events like pandemics, war, or real estate market crashes that can potentially burn your account down. Those are called black swan events—things that happen once every five years or so that you don't see coming. When a black swan event hits, it's newsworthy and history-making. Using put options to protect your account from such events is one level of protection.

In Chapter 3, I went over how to use put options as insurance in detail. The big picture of having insurance comes into play when individual stocks and the overall stock market sells off because of a black swan event and takes your account down with it. This is when put options kick in like an insurance policy and allow you to force someone to buy all your shares of stock at the prices they were before they sold off. This protects your account from major unplanned sell offs. For example, if you have a $100K account, you can buy put options that cover $80K of your account. If the market sold off and your account fell to $50K, it would be made whole again up to $80K. Essentially, you have peace of mind knowing you can never lose more than 20% ($20K in this case) as long as you have that insurance.

It doesn't matter how big or small your account is. You can always take a portion of your money and use it as insurance. Typically, investors with a little more money are going to be excited that they can protect their $100K plus account.

In smaller accounts, investors may not be as excited about protecting their money or it might not be as impactful to their life if they lose that money. You can use a couple of hundred dollars to protect a $4K account, but most investors with a $4K to $10K account level are usually trying to use 100% of that money to grow. Remember, just as with car or home insurance, if a catastrophic event never happens, you're still paying monthly premiums and that money doesn't come back. With smaller accounts in the stock market, it may not make sense to pay a monthly or yearly premium for protection because it can eat into your gains or the amount you have to invest. However, regardless of your account size, there may be other things—like Fed interest decisions or other economic news—that aren't black swan events that you might want protection from.

Put options can be used at any level of account growth but don't usually come into play until your account is larger. It's good to think about it early and be prepared to deploy the strategies as your account grows.

## 3:1 CALL TO PUT AND PUT TO CALL RATIO

If you're bullish on a stock—meaning you believe a stock is going up based on your research and reading the stock chart—and you want to use options to take advantage of it, you can buy call options. But what if you're wrong about the stock and it reverses and goes the other way?

Typically, in that situation you start losing money immediately on your call options. What we teach our students at Power Trades University from a risk management standpoint is to consider adding some put options to minimize risk. Now, you might be thinking if you have both calls and puts, they'll cancel each other out. That's correct but there's a certain mathematical equation that allows for protection in the event that you're totally wrong about the direction the stock is going—and that is the 3:1 ratio. That means for every three call options you buy, you should consider buying one put option. If a stock sells off big and falls by a certain number of dollars, that one put option has the ability to cover what you lose on those three call options or at least minimize the damage.

On the flip side, if that stock goes up like you believe it will, those three calls will more than pay for the cost of the one insurance put—and leave you with profit as well. This insurance strategy means you don't have to be an all or nothing trader. You don't have to be all bullish or all bearish. You can say, "I believe it's going to go up, but if it doesn't, I have my insurance." The sweet spot is the 3:1 ratio. By deploying this strategy, you'll have more piece of mind while you're investing and drastically reduce the likelihood of blowing up your account.

A 3:1 call to put ratio if you're bullish and believe the stock is going up, or a 3:1 put to call ratio if you're bearish and believe the stock is going down, is one way to protect your assets. It can be used when you're growing your account and can be applied once you've made substantial money. If you're trading single stocks, it's a way to have insurance on each trade rather than your overall account and a way to make sure you live to trade another day if the direction of a trade goes horribly wrong.

Here's a real-life scenario. Let's say you believed a meme stock company like AMC or GameStop was going out of business. You wanted to make money from the stock falling, so you bought three put options and, for insurance, you bought one call option. When those stocks actually went through a short squeeze, the stock prices skyrocketed to unbelievably high levels. This happened, although the company's business model and balance sheet did not support the high stock price valuation. You would have been happy to have that one call option to pay for the puts and then some. Sometimes, wonky things happen and that's what having insurance is about. No one walks out of their house expecting to get into an accident every day, but when it happens, they're glad they have insurance.

A lot of the people involved in that short squeeze played a zero-sum game. They either made a killing or lost it all. But if you had the 3:1 put to call ratio on your side, you would have made more money by being wrong than being right, thinking the companies were going out of business. There's power in knowing how to protect your assets and not being 100% convinced that a stock is going to move in one direction.

You want to look at trading in the stock market as a risk manager, not a prophetic genie. The risk manager asks, "What if I'm wrong? Will I live to trade another day? Have I protected my assets?" The gambler says, "If this bet hits, I'm rich," and never thinks about what will happen if they're wrong. The gambler thinks every stock is going to the moon, is often wrong, and is never prepared for being wrong. The risk manager—regardless of how often they're right—is always prepared for being wrong.

## PROTECTING YOUR ACCOUNT USING STOP-LOSS TRIGGERS

No matter how much money you have in your account, making and losing money is an emotional thing. You need to have some protection from your emotions. This is where using stop-loss triggers comes in. A stop-loss trigger is a pre-set order to sell your stock or option to get out of a trade or investment if you want to automatically stop the account from incurring any other losses. These types of automatic triggers are good for those who may be at work or traveling and don't have immediate access to the internet or a cell phone to get alerted and for those who have a predetermined trading game plan. If you're a person who freezes when a stock or the market moves against you, the automatic stop-loss can kick in and sell your position for you, even if you're mentally paralyzed and can't execute on your plan.

Knowing where to set your stop-loss is highly dependent on knowing your "I'm Wrong" level. Remember, it's a level based on technical analysis of the chart where you determine if the stock does this or moves this much in the opposite direction, then sell automatically. This stops the loss, stops the bleeding, and gets you out of the trade.

If you have a $100K trading account, maybe your "I'm Wrong" level gets triggered when you're down $10K. It's better to reset and take the small loss and have $90K to apply to your next investment than to watch your account dwindle to zero in a trade or investment. Getting out with an automatic sell trigger will allow you to cut the emotional attachment cord. This gives you time to clear your head while you consider your next move rather than risk that $90K on a trade that's no longer in the pattern you once thought it was. Setting your stop-loss can also be based on a maximum amount you're willing to risk and lose. Or, as we suggest to our students, set the stop-loss based on support and resistance from the stock chart.

Good times for good companies don't always last. Some companies we think will never go under do. Look at Sears. They were the great American department store. No one thought they were going anywhere. When online shopping became popular, they started closing stores left and right and eventually sold the naming rights to their iconic Sears Tower in Chicago. As I am writing this, it's now called the Willis Tower.

Having an "I'm Wrong" level and a stop-loss trigger to automatically sell and get out of the trade will protect you from your emotions—hoping and praying a stock will turn around after it clearly has decided not to.

## GET STOCK AT A DISCOUNT EVERY TIME OR GET PAID FOR TRYING

Most investors are not aware there are also ways to protect your account on the front end before you enter into a trade. How do you come into a trade or investment with a margin of error? There are several strategic ways to do so using options.

One way to do this is to sell a covered put on a stock. I call this method the "get a stock at a discount or get paid for trying every time" method. This strategy is the art of having the money to buy a stock immediately, but instead of buying it outright you enter into a contract to agree to buy it within a certain time frame—a day, week, or month. You'll get paid up front for agreeing to buy it, which is what you're doing when you sell a covered put.

Here's an example: If you're going to buy Tesla stock at $300 a share and Tesla falls $10 to $290 after you buy it, you're immediately down $10 a share. However, instead of buying Tesla stock immediately, you can sell a covered $300 strike price put. When you sell a covered put it says, "I'm willing to enter into an agreement where you have the right to sell me your Tesla stock between now and (let's say) thirty days for three hundred dollars a share. But for that right, you're going to pay me ten dollars per share." That means you get paid to buy Tesla at $300. So, getting paid that $10 up front provides a $10 cushion.

If Tesla falls $10 from $300 to $290, you would technically own it at $290 if you were forced to buy it because you got paid $10 up front. You come in with a $10 cushion or $10 worth of insurance per share. If you bought the stock outright and it fell $10, you'd be down $10 per share. If you sold the covered put, the buyer of that put can force you to buy the Tesla shares at $300 even though it's worth $290, but since you were already paid that $10 up front, you're now at break-even—whereas the person who bought the stock out right is down $10.

What happens if the stock goes up? This is where you get the stock at a discount or get paid for trying. You get to keep that $10 per 100 shares you were paid for entering the put option contract. If Tesla goes up from $300 to $315 for example, no one is going to force you to buy their shares for $300 a share. You see, as the stock goes to $315, they're up $15 on the shares they own. Even if you subtract the $10 they paid you when they bought the put option contract, they would still be up $5 net.

Now, you may be thinking—why would someone do that? Earlier we talked about how you can protect your account from major losses by buying a put option on single stocks or your whole portfolio. This person is protecting themselves in case Tesla stock falls below $300 by buying a $10 put option—aka insurance policy—that covers them for 30 days. To think of it another way, that person wants to make sure they can't lose any more money past $290 should the stock fall lower in the next 30 days and they're willing to pay $10 per contract for that insurance.

So, essentially, you either buy the stock at a discount or you get paid for trying every time. It's a way of protecting yourself because you're getting money up front. If the stock goes up it doesn't matter, because you got paid just for trying to buy it. Obviously, you miss out on the upside of the stock if it goes higher. However, if it goes lower, you've built in protection upfront before you even own the stock if you have to own it at all.

## THE RENTAL INCOME STRATEGY—SELLING COVERED CALLS

The second way to make money and reduce your risk is by getting paid on shares you already own. If you own at least 100 shares of a stock, you can sell call options against every set of 100 shares you own. This is what I like to call the rental income strategy. You're selling someone the right to buy your stock from you in the future at the current price or a higher. You're covered because you own the stock if it hits that higher price and gets called away from you.

Sticking with the Tesla example, if you own 100 shares of Tesla at $300, you could sell someone a $310 call option. The buyer has the right or the option to buy the stock from you at $310 at some point in the future, let's say 30 days, and for that right they will pay you $10 per share up front. You own the stock and sell a covered call. You're covered because you have the shares. That means if the stock goes above $310 within 30 days, they'll call you and say, "You owe me the stock at $310." And you won't have to worry about where you'll get the stock from and at what price because you already own it.

Say you sell that covered call and bring in that $10 per share.

Again, if the stock drops to $290, that person isn't going to call and ask you to sell it to them at $310—they could buy it on the open market for less. But you still brought in $10 worth of cushion per share on something you already own.

If the stock goes above $300 but not above $310, you get to keep the $10 per share and the stock. Obviously if the stock goes above $310 you don't make any more money and the shares will 100% be called away from you. However, think about it like this—if you own the stock at $300 and get paid $10 up front to sell the stock at $310— if it gets there—it's almost as if you locked in profit up to $320. If it hits $310 and you're forced to sell it, you make the difference between $300 and $310 which is $10, plus you keep the $10 from the option contracts you sold. That's $20 profit—as if the stock had gone to $320. So, essentially, you don't make any money past the stock rising above $320 per share.

This is where options become beautiful. There are so many ways to use them to protect your account. You can buy a put option and protect your portfolio or individual stock trades. If you have stock, you can sell a covered call and rent your stock out. If you want to buy into a stock, you can sell a covered put and get it at a discount or get paid for trying. There are other advanced options strategies we teach inside

Power Trades University, but these three alone will take your trading and investment game to a level above most retail traders' and financial advisors' knowledge.

No matter which strategy you use—if any at all—if you're going to invest, you still need to have an "I'm Wrong" level. When buying a put option for insurance, your "I'm Wrong" level may be the level at which you want to buy the put option coverage. Again, if Tesla is trading at $300 and you say "I'm Wrong" if it falls below $270, you may want to buy a $270 strike price put to ensure your stock doesn't lose value past that.

With the covered put, although you may take in some money upfront—in the example we used, you will take in a $10 cushion—you still need to know your "I'm Wrong" level if the stock falls beyond the $10 cushion. Likewise, with the covered call, if you get paid $10 up front but your $300 stock is starting to fall more than $10 dollars, you still need to know your "I'm Wrong" level. That way, you get out or deploy a different strategy like buying put options to stop the bleeding. With options, you have a way to protect your account no matter what the market throws at you. You can't protect it from not losing money at all, but you can protect yourself and your account from blowing up and watching it go to zero.

That's the power of understanding how options and these strategies work—you're essentially guaranteeing you can live to trade another day.

I often smile when people say, "I heard options are risky." Options are a way to reduce risk. If you remove those strategies, then all you have to go on is hoping the stock goes up. But the market doesn't just go up—we all know stocks and the market can go sideways and down.

The next time someone tells you that options are risky, you'll know they aren't educated as to how options work. Ask them if they think having car insurance is risky, or homeowners' insurance, or life insurance—because they're buying put options every time they pay those insurance premiums , and so are you.

## PROTECTING YOUR ACCOUNT THROUGH STOCK MARKET DIVERSIFICATION

Another strategy for protecting your assets while investing is through diversification. Instead of buying individual stocks, you can buy the top-rated 500 stocks in the S&P 500 by buying the SPY ETF. An ETF is an exchange-traded fund that has a collection of stocks based on sector or industry. The power in buying an ETF like the SPY is that there's protection in the fact that you have the top-rated 500 U.S. stocks. ETFs save you time from researching individual stocks and reduces exposure to any single stock going through a rough time. The SPY is made up of 11 sectors that make up the S&P 500. If one stock or one sector is having a bad day, week, or month, you have other sectors that may hold up.

Additionally, from the standpoint of protecting your assets, most people are afraid of investing and losing all their money. The only way you'll lose all your money investing in the SPY is if the top 500 companies in the U.S. all go out of business in a relatively short period of time. That has a very low probability of happening. The world would probably be ending at that point, and if that was the case, the stock market would be the last thing you'd be worried about.

## HOW TO PROTECT YOUR MONEY ONCE YOU MAKE A LOT OF IT

You must have the mindset of a financial manager or a risk manager to know when it's time to take some chips (money) off the table. When I made over $400K in one trade, some people might have advised, "Oh, leave that in the stock market. You can make so much more money." But the market has inherent risks, and nothing is guaranteed. You have to remember why you're doing this—it's not to watch numbers go up and down in a digital bank account. The goal is to use this money to make a difference out here in the real world and change your real life.

For me, in that trade, another way of protecting and diversifying my assets was taking that money off the table and paying off another asset. I paid off what was left on my mortgage and added another asset to my portfolio. That $400K was protected because a house worth $800K is not going to drop in value to $0. I secured the asset that provides me shelter and peace of mind. There are no more payments, so if something does go drastically wrong, no bank can come after me and take my home. If we need to sell the house, that's a huge chunk of money to help us get on our feet again.

I also have a HELOC on our house. It's a fixed, open line of credit, so if I did go broke, I could borrow against the house up to that fixed amount. That's about half the value of the house. It's an open line of credit without a bunch of hoops to jump through. It's like borrowing money from myself. I don't need to go to a bank and apply after the initial approval. I essentially can play bank with myself. I don't need any outside opinions on what I can use the money for, and I don't have to submit a business plan or pay stubs or tax returns to pull the money out. I can look in the mirror and say, "Self, I need some money."

A note for protecting your assets in the market and in other industries: The best time to apply for lines of credit like the HELOC is when you don't need it. That's when financial institutions are willing to give it to you. The bank is willing to loan you money based on your ability to pay it back. If they think you're in financial trouble or can't submit pay stubs because you lost your job, they're less likely to extend you credit. When you need credit, no one wants to give it to you. It's important to have those protections in place while you're making money and not in a stressful financial place.

## GROWING YOUR PORTFOLIO TO PROTECT YOUR ASSETS THROUGH ASSET ALLOCATION

Initially, you want to focus on mastering one investment vehicle. Most people who are starting out don't have enough time, money, or resources to master investing in multiple industries—e.g., the stock market, real estate, small business, etc. I believe the first goal should be to master the stock market for several reasons. I touched on this earlier, but your money can work for you while you're still working your full-time job. As your account grows, you can pay off smaller debts like credit cards and graduate into paying off other debts, like student loans.

One set of asset allocation could be using your stock market earnings for a down payment on other assets like a rental property. Another asset allocation would be to invest with some of the best companies in the world. Take advantage of their products, intellect, teams, and infrastructure without any of the headache or capital needed to run a business or start a Fortune 500 company yourself. This way, you participate in any upside profits as a shareholder or option trader. Essentially, an Apple Inc. CEO and all their employees and stores can work for you without your having to figure out how to build an iPhone. You do this by being a shareholder or controlling shares with options.

As you invest in the stock market, you may use some of the protection strategies with options I mentioned earlier. As your account grows, you may want to start looking into diversification through other asset classes outside the stock market. For example, you may want to look at life insurance as an investment vehicle, or real estate—both single family and multifamily homes. You may want to investigate investing into businesses that are franchises like a McDonald's.

When I first started looking for investment opportunities, I told myself that one day I wanted to own a McDonald's. That meant I had to get roughly $1.3 million to buy one. The price may be even higher now. What's nice about the stock market is that you can own a piece of the McDonald's empire either by buying the stock or controlling the stock with options without having to come up with millions.

As your income grows, you may want to transition into owning a franchise as a means of diversification and perhaps use the stock market to earn the money to buy one. The thing about owning business systems and real estate is you can pass them down to your family or others who can easily manage them with no technical skills. Learning how to trade and invest in the stock market is a personal skill that's not easily passed on to your family. However, if your family is interested, it's knowledge that—with the right exposure—can last and benefit generations to come.

Any and all investments cost money. However, in the stock market you can get started with a nominal amount and no credit and then transition into other assets later. Now that you have some idea of how to accumulate and protect your assets, you have other styles of investing to look forward to in the future.

Let's talk about some tools to help you learn faster, implement quicker, and get the accountability you need to be successful long term in the market.

**CHAPTER 8: TAKEAWAYS**

- Protect your assets.
- The magic ratio is 3:1.
- Use stop-losses to minimize risk.
- Buy stock at a discount or get paid for trying.
- Rent out stock you own and get paid monthly.
- Diversify your investments through ETFs.

CHAPTER 9

# The Path and Tools to Success

**When trying anything new, there** are going to be challenges. It's easy to quit—people do it all the time. As I mentioned earlier, when I was down and had lost that quarter of a million dollars, I kept asking myself, "What would Warren Buffett do? If he quits, he never becomes Warren Buffett." This is a mental strategy called "the hero's journey." When you're down in the mental dumps and can't see or think clearly, you think about someone who is your hero in the industry you're trying to succeed in. Ask yourself what they would do. I decided at that moment not to quit. If I quit then I'd never become Jason Brown or, shall I say, I'd never get to find out who Jason Brown could become with respect to the stock market.

Once I decided not to quit, I reflected on how I achieved success in the early days with my cousin. Our trades went much better when we were working together, doing the research together, sharing information, and holding each other accountable.

I also thought back to a time when I was overly excited about the opportunity to make money. When I was in network marketing, I spent countless hours over several years trying to build an MLM business but was not making any money doing that. I reflected on what kept me going for so long when I wasn't profiting off it.

What it eventually came down to was what the group gave me. They provided coaching, support, and community. It was my commitment to my dreams and goals and to my peers in the group that I didn't want to let down. The community gave me a place to belong even when things weren't going well. It also gave me a place to dream and receive mental support to keep going.

Once you've had some success and then lose it, you naturally start to question yourself. I would ask myself, "Do you really know what you're doing? Were you just lucky the first time around?" There's a saying that you don't really understand a thing until you can teach the thing. I picked that up in college in our math classes where we had to show the work and then teach back how we got to the answer. In those moments, you really have to understand the problem and the solution backward and forward.

When I looked at the stock market, I thought, "What if I take the same approach?" One of the best ways to know if I truly understood the stock market would be to teach it. As I started to work on making my money back, I decided I would teach what I'd learned from losing big money and what I'm learning along the way from making it back. It would serve as a form of accountability.

If I was teaching people why they should get out of a trade, then I should get out of the trade if I was in it. If I was explaining to other people why it was a good time to get in, then I wanted to be in a trade I really believed in—one I'd be willing to put my own money behind.

Sharing and teaching about the stock market became a system of checks and balances for me, a way to make sure I was practicing what I was preaching. It led me to think about how many other people like me were out there. People who had made money, lost money, needed a place to re-sharpen their skills without feeling shame—a place where they could connect and get support when things weren't going right.

We all want to turn and talk to our best friend or a family member when things aren't going right, but if they're not in the stock market, they're usually the worst people to talk to when things aren't going well. When you share that you lost money or are down in a trade with people who don't understand investing or trading and taking calculated risk, they respond with, "That's why I don't invest in the stock market." Or, "That's why I work and don't even fool with stocks." And you nod and say, "That's why I don't talk to you about trading or investing." It doesn't make them a bad person, just a bad person to talk to about trading or investing. But you still need that outlet, your tribe, your people.

I wanted to know where my people were who knew about trading and investing. I wanted to find my community of people who also needed someone to talk to about what they were seeing in the charts. Since I couldn't find it, I decided to build it.

I knew how important courses and community are, and I was ready to be the teacher behind the courses. Another component I found to be necessary was coaching. Having a coach can help you apply what you've learned and keep you accountable. Coaches also help you think clearly and strategize when things aren't going right.

I wanted to be a coach who was trading his own money. There are coaches out there who teach about investing or trading, but they don't do it themselves. They have no skin in the game. It's different when you're in the game as a coach and are actually playing on the field versus watching it from the sidelines.

These three components—courses, coaching, and community—are the big three Cs for success regardless of whether you're in investing or trading in the stock market.

## COURSES, COACHING, AND COMMUNITY

Whenever people ask me what it takes to be successful or how to get started, I talk about the three Cs. I always present them in the same order—courses, coaching, and community. It isn't enough to have one by itself. You need all three of them. You need them in that order. Like the phrase, "You have to learn to crawl before you can walk and walk before you can run," the three Cs are a prescribed path to success in investing.

With courses, you learn what you need to know about the market. Traders and investors need to understand the game they're playing, the risk, reward, how to spot a good or bad stock, how to enter and exit a trade, etc. Some people come out the gate gambling with no real knowledge. It's all fun and games when you're winning, but eventually if you don't know what you're doing, the house usually wins.

You want to think about the stock market as a profession, not as a Las Vegas casino. In life, if you want to move into a new profession—doctor, lawyer, engineer—you understand that you have to go to school, take courses, study, and learn. The stock market is no different—if we're going to do something we've never done before, we need to study how it works and understand the ins and outs of the profession. The good news is the stock market doesn't take five years and $50K to $100k of debt to learn if you find a program that's well put together.

The stock market—like real estate or becoming a doctor—has its own language and terminology. Sure, it's not as complicated as learning all the parts of a human body, but you need to understand how the market communicates, the terms publicly traded companies use, how analysts talk about publicly traded companies, and how online brokerages use terms for buying, selling, and settling your profitable and losing trades. Can you imagine if you were selling a stock you meant to buy and buying a stock you meant to sell? This can happen if you don't understand the language and programming of the trading platform. As you get educated, the next key is to practice, but you can't practice what you don't understand—education is key.

After getting education through courses and practicing, it's time to get some coaching. Coaching around money is key in the beginning and on an ongoing basis for several reasons. So many emotions are tied to money—unworthiness, fear, and greed. A game where you can lose your hard-earned money comes with high stakes and high emotions for many people. This means you need someone to call out your blind spots the same way a marriage coach or a sports coach will. You definitely need someone who isn't connected to your investment account to look at things objectively outside of the emotional and financial attachment. A coach can help you when you get stuck studying the material, help you develop a gameplan to hit your goals, walk with you as you move toward your goals, and keep you on track and away from shiny object syndrome.

Many professions have internships, apprenticeships, and residencies. These are programs that help coach people to apply what they've learned in their educational programs and courses. Since the stock market can be used as a stream of income, learning the ins and outs should be treated the same as any other career and vocation program. This means studying under someone who has had success in the field you're trying to go into. Some internships or residencies are nonpaid, which means you pay by sacrificing your time.

Learning the stock market is similar to internships that require you to put in the time without getting paid upfront. In the beginning, profits may not be raining down on your bank account as you learn, but if you're looking to build wealth through investing, the upfront sacrifice is worth it for the long-term—or shall I say lifetime—benefits. The difference between getting a stock market coach and a traditional internship is that you might be paying a coach for that internship-style opportunity or mentorship. However, if that coach can get you on your way to making money faster or losing less than you would by investing and trading alone, then it's all win-win. You don't want to get stuck in the learning phase. You want to get into the confidently making money stage as quickly and safely as possible.

How do you pick the right coach? Just as you'd research which school to go to, you'll do the same for coaches and programs. Look at the reviews from students. Look into the reputation of the coach and/or organization. Look at their free content. Is it easy to understand?

Are you finding value in it? Does the teacher help you accomplish what you want to do?

You need community, too. These might be study groups. Some places of work have unions, employee support-and-resource groups, and smaller teams within an office that have a sub-community of their own.

In the stock market, you need a community of like-minded traders. And I don't mean other investors and traders doing the exact same thing and supporting bad behavior like some of the meme stock and gambling forums. You want a community of people who have the same values and principles, who trade the same way you trade, and who follow similar principles and can hold you accountable.

A paid community where everyone has studied the same or a similar course is going to have a much different feel and level of traders than a free random one that accepts everyone. It does you no good if you go to a free social media forum or community and everyone in there is chasing meme stocks, no one knows the difference between a high-probability and low-risk trade, and they look at the stock market as a game of luck and chance. If that's not your style of trading—and I hope it isn't—then you're not going to get much value from being in that room.

Similarly, if you're trying to become a millionaire in five years, it doesn't help much to talk to the guys in the 401K forum who only contribute monthly sums and hope it grows to a nice retirement fund over 40 years. They aren't going to know what you're talking about or understand what you're doing in the market. The key here is not to slam other groups but to help you understand that a community is only as good as the information the other traders have, the style they've been trained on, and how similar the goals of the individuals in the group are. So, it's not about joining just any group or community but to join a community that's trading in the style and trying to accomplish the goals you're trying to accomplish.

## THE POWER TRADE FRAMEWORK

Courses are the first step I recommend on this trading journey. Digital courses offer incredible flexibility to get the information on the go. The way we structure our courses is so that the lessons build on each other and each course builds on the previous one. When I was the one going through books, trying to learn this stuff, all the books were going over my head and I felt like I needed to get another book to understand what they were talking about in the first book.

I wanted someone to show me what they were talking about and show me what they meant. That's why I went the route of teaching the courses through video rather than only through books, PDFs, and blogs. Although we offer PDFs as supplemental learning instructions, I know how important it is to be shown. It's important to see how to open an account and what it looks like when you make your first trade. When you can see what you're supposed to do—see what it looks like to buy and sell—it removes the fear of the unknown. With a video format you can pause, rewind, rewatch, and make sure you get it.

When it comes to giving and receiving coaching, I believe the format should be structured so that students can get near real-time feedback as well as insights as to how to apply what's being taught in the actual market and current environment. When I read books, I would read about hypothetical situations or theories on investment strategies that were applied in a different era. I often felt the market had changed from the style of investing the books described. I wanted real-time coaching and strategies that work in the current market.

The way we structure coaching fits the current time and place in the market. The examples in our courses come and go as the stock market changes. I want people in the coaching sessions to see how to apply information in real time with current companies within current market conditions.

Before you can trade live, you need to first have that fundamental understanding of how things work. You can't be coached if you don't understand the basics—that's why courses come first. Coaching is live, in real time, and shows how to apply what's learned in the courses to the current market conditions. The information has to be current. How does it work today in a post-COVID-19, high-inflation environment, as opposed to back in the Great Depression or in 2008 when the housing market crashed? My coaches and I work with my Power Trades members live so we can figure it out together.

All the trades we find during our live sessions go into a spreadsheet that can be accessed at any time by any member. You can read about which stocks we talked about, where we think they're going, and what option play we're thinking about. Every session is recorded with time stamps so you can also watch the replay in case you missed it live.

When I was putting together the programs inside Power Trades University, I worked to remove the main excuses that most people have: I don't have time, I don't have the money, I don't have the knowledge. I remember taking courses from other coaches and having questions or wanting feedback about a stock that wasn't discussed in the course.

I didn't have anywhere to go to talk to someone or a place to go to get answers. I wanted the ability to get my questions answered. I also wanted a platform that wasn't reliant on time zones. So, I built what I wished I'd had. I designed a platform with a community forum where you can connect with other traders 24 hours a day, 7 days a week.

## IF SOMETHING GOES WRONG

I see examples all the time of traders who could have avoided some major mistakes if they'd had courses, coaching, and community. One extreme example was a young, novice trader who made news headlines using the online trading platform Robinhood several years back. He put all his money into an options trade that went bad, and his account allegedly went to negative $730K. He thought he owed that much money and became so distraught that he committed suicide.[5] My heart goes out to his family.

He's the perfect example of not having the three Cs. His first fail was not having access to courses, because if he understood how options and the stock market worked, he wouldn't need coaching or community to figure out he didn't owe that much money. If he'd had the right education, he might have avoided that strategy or understood the risk versus reward ratio better. More important, he would've known that he wouldn't be on the hook for that much money and would probably still be alive today.

---

5   Sergei Klebnikov and Antoine Gara, "20-Year-Old Robinhood Customer Dies by Suicide After Seeing a $730,000 Negative Balance," *Forbes*, June 17, 2020, https://www.forbes.com/sites/sergeiklebnikov/2020/06/17/20-year-old-robinhood-customer-dies-by-suicide-after-seeing-a-730000-negative-balance/?sh=788280681638.

Imagine if he'd had a coach as well as those courses. He could reach out to his coach and say, "Hey, am I reading this right? Am I on the hook for $730K?" A coach could have coached him not to take those trades or told him not to use a strategy he wasn't ready for. A coach could have helped him devise a strategy with less risk if he was determined to get into that trade. A coach could also have showed him that he was not on the hook for that large amount and not to panic. At the end of the day, he was not responsible for owing that much money, it just appeared that he did until the complete trade settled.

Allegedly, he did try to reach out to Robinhood, but his emails went unanswered and there was no direct customer service number to reach out to at the time. Most free-trading discount brokerage companies don't staff call centers or provide a way to reach out to them for immediate support. They have automated email responses. They want everything going through their app. But what if that young man had had a coach or community of competent traders to reach out to—he would have gotten answers or at least have been pointed in the right direction. A community could have advised him about what he should do and could have been there for him when his messages to Robinhood went unanswered.

Most people don't go to the extreme of committing suicide, but many people live in quiet desperation when a trade goes against them and they're unsure how to unwind it, repair it, or get out of it. They take a loss and have no one to talk to about being depressed, not sleeping well at night, or being anxious about their finances and their next move. There are many levels of anxiety that people who don't have access to courses, coaches, or a community experience.

One young woman reached out to me through Instagram @brownreport with a question about an option trade she was in. She was part of another community and I asked why she didn't talk to them. She said they made her feel stupid for asking questions. When she explained their conversations, I told her it seemed like they were responding that way because they didn't understand her questions or how the stock market really works. Because they didn't understand, they couldn't answer, and they didn't want to admit they didn't know the answer.

I immediately saw what they were doing. It's a repercussion of having the wrong coach or community. When a bad coach who doesn't really know what they're doing can't answer a question, their only tactic is to make you feel stupid for asking the question in the first place. If they do that, number one, it's not helpful—you could have gotten a real answer from someone who understands. Number two, it leads to people giving up on the stock market because they're losing money, not getting good support, and not feeling smart enough to make it work. If you get started on the wrong foot in such a beautiful industry and take an unnecessary loss or get scarred, you might end up walking away from something that could have a real positive impact on your life.

The Robinhood trader suffered from not having access to all three Cs. The young woman who reached out to me had bad coaching and a bad community that made her feel stupid. When it comes to community, it's worth the money to pay for a legitimate, vetted trader community. People who decide to join random, unvetted forums and chat rooms don't know if they're talking to a bored 13-year-old or a licensed professional. They don't know how these people's trading methodology developed or where they learned their strategies.

Members of these random communities say things like, "Let's get GameStop. Let's get AMC. Let's get these meme stocks, they're only going to increase in value." And you think, "Okay, these people sound smart." There's no way of vetting, knowing who's behind the screen, or where they got their training. You have no idea if the owner of GameStop himself is in there egging things on—"Yes, this is going to skyrocket tomorrow."

You can join free forums and chatrooms, but there's power in joining a paid platform where people have been vetted and a moderator regulates the posts to make sure they fit the methodology and meet the community guidelines, such as no profanity and no politics unless it relates to a stock or the stock market. A moderator can say, "This is how we think and this is how we trade. Post anything outside of our agreed methods and it will be deleted. You'll be banned for promoting gambling."

There's power in paying for that level of moderation to make sure everyone is on the same page and ensure the integrity of the community, just as you would want to choose an accredited college. That's what we offer at Power Trades University. You get to work with real traders, people who are trained the Power Trade way, and a real community of people abiding by the Power Trade community guidelines. If someone comes in and says, "Hey I'm gonna do this trade," our members will point out if it's not a 1:3 risk versus reward ratio. If someone says "I'm gonna get in this trade, earnings come out tomorrow," our members will say, "We don't trade over earnings." The original poster might still take those trades, but the community responds from a place of shared educational standards and reminds the trader of the risk in breaking the rules.

No matter the course, the coach, or the community, it's still your trading account. You have to make your own decisions, but the three

Cs can sure help when you're getting cocky or too far outside of the trading guidelines.

## SUCCESS WITH THE THREE CS

There was a couple in the Power Trades community who used what they learned in the courses to change their lives. They posted their wins in the community, as everyone is encouraged to do. At times they were making as much as $100 or $200 a day and they were doing it by only putting $500 or $700 at risk.

The numbers might have looked small compared to what we've covered in this book, but they were hitting those 10% returns on smaller trades, and they were doing it two to three times a week. That's like having your money working two to three extra eight-hour shifts a week and bringing you home a paycheck for it.

In my Five-Year Millionaire program, we encourage people to start their trading journey with a $4K trading account. If they have one of those 10% returns once a month for five years or 60 trades, they can become a millionaire. This couple was doing it two to three times a week!

The two of them ended up buying a Tesla, their dream car. They were able to do that with the help of the money they made in the stock market. We were able to help them fund one of their dreams, a dream they didn't think was possible before.

Another member of the community is traveling the world. She's living off her savings, so her goal is to make enough every month in the market to cover her cost of living and travel expenses without dipping into her savings. Based on the program, she's $30K ahead of her goal and her cost of living is a fraction of that. She has the peace of mind that she can keep traveling without risking her savings with the stock market education, coaching, and tools we've given her to help her reach those goals.

When I first started Power Trades University, it was to create a community for myself I couldn't find anywhere else. Now, it's become so much more. I'm literally helping people fund their dreams and start their journeys to becoming millionaires.

Getting rich is not as hard or as complicated as people think. It's all about following a process and a simple plan, but to do that you have to have the right courses, coaching, and community to guide you along the way. That's what this is all about.

**CHAPTER 9: TAKEAWAYS**

- Recalling the "hero's journey" can get you through tough times.
- Your friends and family may not be the best people to talk to about investing.
- The three Cs for success are courses, coaching, and community.
- Picking a community to join should be considered carefully.

# Conclusion

**B**ecoming a millionaire is not about *not* drinking that $6 coffee. Becoming a millionaire starts in your mind before it manifests into its physical form. It's not about skipping that $6 coffee you love unless it's the reason you can't afford to invest in the education to learn how to grow your money and the reason you can't fund your trading account—in which case, give it up. Starting your millionaire journey doesn't have to be about what you're going to stop doing, it's really about what you're going to *start* doing. I recommend you start doing what wealthy people do—they learn how to have their money work hard for them. They learn how to have their money grow and multiply for years to come, usually inside some investment vehicle like the stock market.

The good news is there's no monopoly on the stock market or the information needed to learn—you simply have to decide you're going to do something new with your money. You're going to learn how to have your money work hard for you instead of you always working hard for it. Decide today to do something different with your mind like learning the skill of trading. Do something different with your time, take that course, open that trading account, and get started.

No one is going to take care of your money for you like you.

Why not outsource your investing to a financial advisor or go to your local bank and have them take care of it for you? The reality is no one is going to care about your money or take care of it like you. Investment bankers and financial advisors have a job and a place in this world, but it's usually not to help you become a millionaire. That's *your* job.

When there's opportunity in the stock market, be it daily, weekly, monthly, or yearly, most investment bankers and financial advisors do not have the time, knowledge, or capacity to reach out to every one of their clients and advise on how they can take advantage of current or changing market conditions. They usually have basic strategies that can be deployed across any person's account regardless of its size or an individual's personal goals. All too often it's a good old "buy and hold strategy," a put-a-little-away-every-month and dollar-cost average strategy. When the market is down, most investment bankers and financial advisors are not going to tell you how to capitalize on it with put options or how to protect your account from major sell offs. Usually, you're advised to hold for the long term. Sure, that's a plan, but usually not one for becoming a millionaire and certainly not a plan for becoming a millionaire in five years.

You can do this—it's not as hard as you think.

## CONCLUSION

Becoming a millionaire from the stock market is not as hard as you think. All it takes is a plan—not a plan built on hope and prayer, but a plan based on education, strategy, and consistent action mixed with discipline. The plan begins with deciding you want to become a millionaire from the stock market, getting the right education, then taking action by opening a trading account starting with $4K and placing 60 trades where you make a 10% return. You can spread those 60 trades out over whatever time frame you want, but if you can do one a month for five years, you would be a millionaire at the end of those five years.

Sounds simple enough right? Well, it is, but first you have to get the knowledge, education, and practice to know how to find trades that can yield a 10% return and how to apply the correct option strategies to supercharge those returns. What's important to note is that it's possible, even if you have less than $4K to start—just get started wherever you are. I started with $500. If you've tried trading and investing in the stock market before and it didn't work out, it's never too late to start again with new information, new strategies, and a new set of rules to turn it all around.

If you've gotten this far, my friend, congratulations. You took the first step—a step most people won't take—to seek information on how to become a millionaire. The next step in your journey is to get the right stock market training and coaching so you can open your first account, if you don't already have one and prepare to start your Five-Year Millionaire journey. Start it by building the right habits, the right strategies, and looking for the right trades.

There's a saying that "a smart man learns from his mistakes, but a truly wise man learns from the mistakes of others." You will make some mistakes on your journey, especially if you go at it alone, but I'm hopeful this book has helped you learn from some of mines. If you want to speed up the process and build upon the knowledge from the mistakes I've made and shared in this book, then I'd love to invite you to check out my community. This is a place where you can can get the right education, connect with others who are on the same journey, and get trades sent to you that are designed to give you the return that puts you on a path to becoming a millionaire in five years. You can find out more at powertradesuniversity.com.

Cheers to taking control of your financial future and cheers to becoming a part of the Power Trades Five-Year Millionaire family.

# Acknowledgments

I never thought I would write a book. Maybe that was because every book I read on finance and investing seemed like it was missing something for me to truly connect to. It wasn't until so many people started to say "you have to tell your story" that I thought maybe, just maybe, it was time for me to write the book that I wish I had had when I first got started investing, a story of hope and guidance for regular people. And so here we are.

**My Wife, Audrey Brown**

To my wife, Audrey Brown, you have been through and witnessed many of my ups and down. From seeing me lose all my money and have to move back to my mother's home to witnessing the rebuild and making millions, thank you for supporting me through some of the roughest times, believing in my outlandish visions and for being there to experience some of the most beautiful moments this life has to offer. Thank you for being an awesome mom to our two children, Kayla and Jalen.

### My Kids, Kayla and Jalen

To my kids, Kayla Brown and Jalen Brown. You both inspire me every day. It is such a blessing and a privilege to watch you grow, stay curious, and blossom into beautiful, kind human beings. This book is a blueprint not only for the world, but for you two so that you can look back on our family tree and be able to say, "Right there is where it all changed for our family." I love you both.

### My Mother, Zolda Brown

To my mother, the late Zolda Brown. Thank you for being such a strong woman. Thank you for always putting your kids first. You were the example of hard work, dedication, sacrifice, selflessness, and true love. I pray I can continue to make you proud, and I can only hope to help as many people as you did through your acts of service, love, and kindness.

### My Father, Gerald Brown

To my father, Gerald Brown, who was taken away from us too soon. Without you I literally wouldn't be here.

### My Brother, Gerald Courtney Brown

To my older brother, Gerald Courtney Brown. We may not have seen eye to eye on everything growing up in life, but our relationship has grown and blossomed over the years. Your unique way of pushing me and driving me to greatness has fueled me for a great portion of my life. For the times you quietly said, "I'm proud of you," or the times you would loudly say "No, he's the real big brother." I love you.

## ACKNOWLEDGMENTS

**My Cousin Roney Glenn Jr.**

To my cousin Roney Glenn Jr. We always had a close relationship growing up. You were the first one to truly introduce me to the stock market and stock options, and for that, I am forever grateful. You turned me on to this industry and opened up a whole world that I was able to take to another level. I will forever be grateful for all those early days of charting stocks together, looking at option chains, and doing stock market research. I appreciate all the times you pushed me to experience and enjoy life. Many of the stories in this book would not have happened if it weren't for you.

**My Cousin Kenneth Glenn**

To Kenneth Glenn (not my blood cousin, but my cousin through my cousin Ron Glenn). You have been so instrumental in my life. From the early days of turning Ron and me on to network marketing and the lifelong journey of personal development that followed, I am eternally grateful for you. When I launched the business and secretly hoped no one would buy my stocks and options coaching program so I could say, "See? This doesn't work," the first payment came through for a subscription and it was you, and then I was forced to do the work that was always within me. Without your support there may have never been The Brown Report or Power Trades University. I appreciate you.

**My Best Friend Falonzo Porter**

To my best friend Falonzo (Zo) Porter. We have had a lifetime of fun and cool experiences and being there for each other. Thank you for being there when the business of coaching people in the stock market wasn't going well and I called you on the phone and said, "I'm shutting it all down, it's over." You talked me off the ledge when I wanted to shut the business down, and you supported and witnessed the rebirth and rebuild of the program that has helped so many people. You have lent your ear to listen to all my personal and professional woes as well as my wins. You're like a brother to me for life. Thanks for everything.

**Roney Glenn Sr.**

To Ron Glenn Sr. You have been a father figure to me for all of my life. All the early days of talking to me and sharing your wisdom kept me out of jail and prevented me from committing my life to gangs or doing anything too stupid that might have gotten me locked up. In your profession you worked on burned and broken homes, but your true gift was always working on and speaking life into broken people. Thank you for always stepping up and stepping in.

**To My Cousin Mavis Glenn**

Thank you for always encouraging me and speaking some of the realest words into my soul. You may not remember the time I was stressed and just so tired of all the weight of the world and was ready to drop out of school at Wayne State University and you said "Boy it ain't even about you. You don't know what young black man or who needs to see you walk across that stage to know that they can do it." I have carried that lesson with me throughout my life. When times get tough or things get hard which they will when you are trying to accomplish great things. I am reminded that " this is not about me". It's about all the people it may impact both negatively and positively in the future. Thanks for giving me to the fuel to get across the finish line.

## ACKNOWLEDGMENTS

**My EO Forum Mates (Jenny Feterovich, Joe Lentine, Melissa Hughes, Linda Girard, Rob Coyte, Scott Seltzer)**

To my EO (Entrepreneurs' Organization) forum mates: Jenny Feterovich for always telling me "You got this," Joe Lentine for casually saying, "I'd feel better if you had a book" and planting the seed for me to write one, Melissa Hughes for always reminding me to step into my greatness and choose powerfully, Linda Girard for saying, "This is going to be amazing" any time I share about the book, and Rob Coyte and Scott Seltzer for always being positive and encouraging and supportive in our 5% journeys and on the road to writing this book. Thank you all for always pushing me, encouraging me, and supporting me to reach new heights.

**Book Launchers**

To Julie Broad and the Book Launchers team. Julie, from the first time I met you through our late friend Cindy when you were first moving to America from Canada, every time I saw you, you would say, "You need a book. When's that book coming out?" It might have taken a decade, but it's finally out. I appreciate you, your push to write a book, your team, and your company for the opportunity to work on my book. I can truly say this is a team sport, and I am not sure I would have written or finished this book without your team guiding and pushing me through the entire process.

**My High School, Laura F. Osborn**

To all my Osborn Knights for believing in me and voting me most likely to succeed in the graduating class of 1999. For all the messages of support and encouragement and all that have reached out and said, "I'm proud of you," or "We knew if anyone was going to do something special it was you," and sent me other beautiful words of encouragement. I pray I can continue to positively represent people who come from humble neighborhoods like ours and show that we too can make it out and make an impact on the world.

**Linda and Harold West**

To the late Linda and Harold West. You were the two first Black people I knew to own real estate. You were the first ones to take me to a cottage you owned when I needed some time away from the stresses of life as a kid. You were my first examples of normal people who took education seriously, worked hard, managed money well, and achieved several levels of success. I am forever grateful for your friendship to my mom and how you treated me like a son. You both showed me in real time that it was possible for people who look like me to own something with no special talents, just education, a work ethic, and a game plan. I am truly grateful for the impact you both had on my life.

**My Uncle William Brown**

To my late Uncle Buddy (William Brown), you set the tone of entrepreneurship in the family by owning your own shop, Brown's Collision. I was so proud and inspired to see our name on the building every time I came up to Flint, Michigan. I always looked up to you and enjoyed the many times we spent together where you poured invaluable entrepreneurship knowledge and words of wisdom into me. You aways kept things so simple. I am always reminded of your famous saying, "Tough times don't last, son. Tough people do." Thanks for allowing me to spend time in your great entrepreneurial spirit, which eventually rubbed off on me.

# ACKNOWLEDGMENTS

**My Home Church Family**

To Pastor Porter and Sister Porter and the entire Old Solid Rock Missionary Baptist Church family. Thank you for always keeping me in your thoughts and prayers and helping me build a solid spiritual foundation.

**Makayla Land**

To Makayla Land, my first and longest standing employee at the time of writing this. Thank you for the brilliance, commitment, and dedication that you bring to work every day. Thank you for supporting my dreams and goals as well as all of the process and systems that run behind the scenes. I truly don't know where I would be without your support.

**My Tribe and Following**

To all my Power Traders, Brown Report subscribers, current and future Five-Year Millionaires, and everyone who follows and supports me on social media. It is not easy to put your thoughts, wins, losses, successes, and failures online for the world to see, but I do it in hopes that it can help someone. Your comments, support, shares, and likes fuel me to keep going and continue sharing, and they inspired me to put my work out in the form of a book. Thank you all.

## LET'S KEEP THE
# CONVERSATION GOING

Visit **thebrownreport.com** for more insights on how to master the market and create passive income.

Special order bulk purchases for your company, organization, or community by contacting **info@thebrownreport.com**.

Book Jason for workshops and consultations via **info@thebrownreport.com**.

Book Jason for speaking engagements and podcasts via **info@thebrownreport.com**.

## CONNECT WITH **JASON** AT...

- @TheBrownReport
- @brownreport
- jasonbrown1124
- Podcast: Five Year Millionaire
- @brownreport

## THANK YOU FOR READING!

If you enjoyed *Five Year Millionaire*, please leave a review on Goodreads or on the retailer site where you purchased this book.